W9-CLL-417

DATE DUE			
FEB 7			
FEB 20			

68893
Moran

St. Procopius College Library
Maple Ave. and College Road
Lisle, Illinois

Studies in Religious Education

Edited by
Gerard S. Sloyan
Head, Department of Religious Education
The Catholic University of America

Catechetics or religious education is a theological discipline. It is a part of pastoral theology and is allied to the study of preaching and the study of liturgical celebration. So long as it is dealt with apart from the ways in which God's word is experienced in our midst, so long as it is assumed to be chiefly a matter of social and psychological concern over a message already sufficiently well known, it will not flourish as an activity of the Church. In fact, catechizing is no less than the faithful transmission of the Gospel to the little ones, to adolescents, to the simple, to sophisticated adults. This is a work than can only be done if the Gospel is well known to the catechist, and if even before this the theologian has recognized the need of sharing his findings with the preacher and the teacher for their work of proclaiming and catechizing.

There have been serious limitations put upon the catechetical apostolate in the United States and Canada—needlessly, it would seem —as a result of certain misunderstandings and omissions. The chief misunderstanding centers on the supposition that theology is the province of first-rate intellects, catechetics the concern of men and women of second and third rank. The major omission is the failure to produce a theological literature on the offices of preaching and teaching (*kerygma* and *catechesis*). One needs to have considerable figures in the chairs of catechetics, homiletics, and pastoral care in the major universities if this literature is to come into being. By and large such figures have not been found there. The name Sailer comes to mind from the last century, Arnold, Grasso, Goldbrunner, Jungmann, Pfliegler from this; with them the litany is almost complete. The result is that an enterprise of popular exposition has gone ahead either without roots in scholarship or in virtue of such adaptations of scholarship as the working apostle (whether preacher or teacher) was capable of. The latter had the burden of transforming the conclusions of the theological disciplines into categories suitable for his own purposes. Often, he was incapable of this task, and so the job did not get done. Pulpit proclamation and classroom explanation continued in the old ways because the supposition was false which supposed that the practitioner could do his own adaptation of scholarly materials. Even the impressive *haute vulgarisation* that has marked our times is insufficient for the purpose. Men tend to think particularly. If a work geared especially to their needs has not been done they tend to think nothing has been done at all. More to the point, they are likely never to hear what has been done. The scholarly labors that should have proved helpful to them simply never came to their attention.

For all these reasons the firm of Herder and Herder is launching a series of "Studies in Religious Education." The need is pastoral; the response to the need in this case is scholarly. A vast catechetical enterprise without matching resources of theological and socio-psychological research is a perilous venture, and must come to an end. The series begins with two volumes by Gabriel Moran, F.S.C., on the theology of revelation and the implications of this fact of Christian life for a fruitful catechesis. As it progresses the series will include titles which will be concerned chiefly with theology, with cultural anthropology, or with psychology. The major interest of a particular author, however, should not mean a lack of balance among the elements necessary for an effective approach to the catechetical problem.

It is to preserve such balance that the series is being inaugurated.
—G. S. S.

THEOLOGY OF REVELATION

Theology of Revelation

Gabriel Moran, F.S.C.

Theodore Lownik Library
Illinois Benedictine College
Lisle, Illinois 60532

HERDER AND HERDER

231.74
M795t

1966
HERDER AND HERDER NEW YORK
232 Madison Avenue, New York 10016

Nihil obstat: Brendan W. Lawlor
                 Censor Deputatus
Imprimatur: Patrick C. Brennan
                 Vicar General, Diocese of Burlington
                 December 2, 1965

The *Nihil obstat* and *Imprimatur* are official declarations that a book or pamphlet is considered to be free of doctrinal or moral error. No implication is contained therein that those who have granted the *Nihil obstat* and *Imprimatur* agree with the contents, opinions, or statements expressed.

Library of Congress Catalog Card Number: 66–16578
© 1966 by Herder and Herder, Incorporated
Manufactured in the United States of America

68893

Contents

Preface

THEOLOGY that is alive is intimately connected with the needs and problems of the Christian people, the Church. The theologian is at the service of the community. He is not a solitary student devoted to the pursuit of his own intellectual satisfaction, but a man engaged with others in a task arising from the contemporary situation of the community to which he belongs and for which he works. His task is to help the community reach that reflexive understanding of Christian truth which is demanded for the full and fruitful living of the Christian life at a particular time. Christians do not live in a timeless isolation. Particular times have particular problems. No generation has exactly the same mentality as the generations that went before. Unless faith is insulated from life and rendered sterile, Christians have continually to appropriate Christian truth afresh, not change but rethink their beliefs and gain a new understanding of the revelation of God in Christ. That revelation is a reality always present. Since it is fundamentally an interpersonal communion, its formulation in concepts and words is not primary. But such a formulation is an essential moment in the appropriation of revelation by the community, and the work of the theologian in focusing and formulating the awareness he discerns and shares within the Church is indispensable.

An urgent pastoral problem at the moment is to provide Christians with a better understanding of the meaning of revelation itself. Some may find this statement an exaggeration.

11

I do not think it is. Christians are living among people for whom the concept of revelation is meaningless. The secular world may admire some of Christian teaching, but it does not take seriously the idea of a revelation from God. To leave Christians faced with this challenge without an adequate, satisfying concept of revelation is to paralyze and endanger their faith. Such a defect blocks the unfolding of the faith in their minds and in their lives. They suffer from a radical uneasiness—a more common state than many are willing to admit. The fact is that the concept of revelation purveyed by the average manual is inadequate. Theologians have been more concerned to argue for the existence of revelation than to analyse what revelation means. Happily, theology is now busily repairing past defects. The *Constitution on Divine Revelation* of the Second Vatican Council will be a powerful stimulus to further effort. It has already made clear that the ecumenical problem of the relation between Scripture and tradition can be tackled effectively only by discussing the nature of revelation itself.

Against this background I warmly welcome this book of Brother Gabriel Moran. Not only does he make recent thought on the subject available to American and English readers, but his work is a valuable contribution to present discussions. His own exposition is clear and readable, and so I shall not delay the reader by a summary of what he says. I should like, however, to express my great satisfaction with his presentation of revelation as the interpersonal union between God and men within the history of a community, with his understanding of the man Jesus as the recipient of the total revelation, so that the consciousness of Christ becomes central in the revelational order, with the stress the author lays on the continuing revelatory action of Christ, and, finally, with his balanced awareness that the objections to a "propositional revelation" must not be met by decrying knowledge but by a deeper appreciation of the pre-conceptual level in knowledge. There is much more in the book, and other points may strike other readers. They should not be afraid to ask further questions, because the book is part of an ongoing discussion. But I am sure they will share my gratitude to Brother Moran for having opened out so important a subject.

I am looking forward to reading the promised sequel, which will apply this theology of revelation to the problems of catechetics.

CHARLES DAVIS

Introduction

THERE are a number of skills in happy conjunction here which make this study the important one it is. One comes from the fact that the author is a trained philosopher who was lecturing in that discipline while he did theological study. The chief weakness in certain theologians whose orientation is biblical is an impatience with or downright ignorance of philosophical ways of thinking. This can disqualify them from the theologian's task.

A second gift the author possesses derives from his unremitting concern to say things meaningfully for the hearer. His religious congregation is made up of teachers in Christian schools. Like any good teacher he is ill at ease until the shibboleth, the verbal convention, has stopped masking meaning or substituting for thought process and begun to convey ideas, to communicate adequately the struggle that went into their formulation.

A final qualification enabling the author to do a work of this sort is his concern with living language. The Bible is a monument of speech proper to the times in which it was produced. Some of this contemporaneous quality lives on; much dies. To deal with the religious needs of the men who live after Bible times one must have clear vision as to which among the patterns of human life and language survive and which cannot hope to survive. Our revelation will forever have been biblical, while at the same time it cannot come to the men of any given age in precisely biblical categories. Sensitivity to the virtues and the limitations of a revelation that was made in ancient times marks every page of this study. The author knows that God's word must come to men in a perpetual dialectic of *then* and *now* or it will never come at all.

Particularly, one welcomes the serious attention given to a theology of revelation in a context of religious education. Theology is a sterile science unless its explorations and conclusions become the possession of the common man. Preaching and catechizing are the ordinary ways of the spread of the Gospel, whether they be done orally or by way of journalism and publication. Too often theologians have written for other theologians, not simply as it happened but on principle. This narcissism of thought is lamentable. It was seldom conscious snobbery. Invariably it arose from the conviction that the work of translation into everyday categories of speech was someone else's work—a creature less than the theologian. Actually, no theologian dwells on the heights unless he is capable of taking on the task of communicating. He is not Olympian from the fact that he cannot be in touch with ordinary mortals; he becomes so only when he can.

There are several roles in combination in the author of this volume: the non-cleric and the theologian, the theologian and the educator, the educator and the stylist, the stylist and the man. We are fortunate to have an exposition such as this from a writer so gifted.

GERARD S. SLOYAN

Author's Introduction

ON Tuesday, November 20, 1962, at the first session of Vatican Council II a majority of bishops voted to reject the schema, "The Sources of Divine Revelation," that had been drawn up by the preparatory commission. This vote, together with the approval of Pope John XXIII, ended debate on the schema and returned it to a commission headed by Cardinals Alfredo Ottaviani and Augustin Bea. That date and that action, according to one of the Church's leading theologians, "will be recognized in the history of the Church as marking the definitive close of the counter-Reformation, because on that day the Council Fathers by a majority vote rejected a document that was too little ecumenical and too inspired by an anti-Protestant Catholicism."[1]

A new text of the schema was prepared by April 22, 1963. Following additional suggestions from the bishops the schema was again revised and reissued on July 3, 1964. In this form it reached the Council floor during the third and fourth sessions for final changes before its promulgation on November 18, 1965. In the following chapters I shall deal with many of the individual points within this constitution. Here I merely note two changes that occurred in the multiple revisions of this document: 1) the original title, "The Sources of Divine Revelation," was replaced by the simpler title, "Divine Revelation"; 2) the introductory section on the nature of revelation was expanded to become Chapter I in the final revision.

[1] Yves Congar, as quoted in "La schéma sur la Révélation," in *Documentation Catholique*, LXI (November 1, 1964), cols. 1393–1394.

These two changes, at first sight rather trifling, are symbolic of the major change that has taken place and continues to take place in Catholic thinking on the nature of revelation. The Second Vatican Council can be viewed on the one hand, as approving and as bringing to definite formulation these theological developments concerning revelation. On the other hand, the work of Vatican II, as that of the councils before it, can also be understood as the beginning of further theological reflection. Far from ending discussion on the nature of revelation, the Council has provided a framework within which more fruitful discussion may now proceed. From what we have said of the Council's work, one thing above all is certain: it is the nature of revelation itself that is now in question. The main issue can no longer be the means of revelation, the organs of transmission, the places where revelation is to be sought. All these questions are legitimate but must be considered secondary. They can be answered only if we have a clear understanding of revelation itself.

To many Catholics, even those not unfamiliar with theology, the proposal to consider the "theology of revelation" may sound a bit strange. In the first place, if one understands that phrase in its most general sense, it would appear that the study of revelation is coextensive with theology. But in that case, any single work claiming to summarize the theology of revelation would be impossible if not absurd. On the other hand, if one understands the phrase in the sense in which it has been used in apologetic treatises of the past century, there would seem to be plenty of these works entitled *De Revelatione.* But were that the case, then a summary of the theology of revelation would seem to be superfluous if not useless.

What I am concerned with in this work, however, is neither the whole of Catholic theology nor the apologetics section of theology. My interest is in the essence or nature of divine revelation. This is an area which is susceptible to examination

18

and is both important for theological analysis and fruitful for pastoral insight. Furthermore, instead of there being an excess of treatises on the subject, there are in fact few Catholic works which fit this category. The real difficulty to be faced is not that this topic is overly extensive or already exhausted, but that the theology of revelation is not yet developed in Catholic circles. In addition to the principles provided by Vatican II there are elements for a synthesis on revelation present in Catholic theology. Little attempt has been made, however, to bring these elements together in an extended and detailed study. An exception is the fine work by René Latourelle, *Théologie de la révélation*.[2] Even in this long study, however, the author claims only to be breaking the ground for more developed works some-day to be written in Catholic theology.[3] Obviously, in this work I cannot pretend to offer a final synthesis on revelation. I would like, nevertheless, to consider some points that I believe are most crucial for the development both of a scientific theology of revelation and of a pastorally relevant understanding of revelation. None of these points is entirely new, but many of them are usually dealt with too briefly and in too much isolation to produce an integrated theological understanding of revelation.

The study of the theology of revelation should be of significance not only to the professional theologian, but to those involved in the pastoral ministry of the Church. The questions raised within this part of theology are so fundamental to Catholic faith that they cannot fail to have profound effects upon preaching and catechizing. This is true despite the fact that the questions raised may seem at first to be abstract and impractical. A deeper penetration of foundational questions has far-reaching effects which are not always immediately evident.

---

[2] René Latourelle, *Théologie de la révélation* (Bruges, Desclée de Brouwer, 1963); there is also a small work by Guardini which is still useful: Romano Guardini, *Die Offenbarung* (Würzburg, Werkbund, 1940); see also Werner Bulst, *Revelation* (New York, Sheed and Ward, 1965).

[3] Latourelle, *op cit.*, p. 14.

In summarizing contemporary theology of revelation the present study should help to reveal theology in the making and to indicate that the theological struggling with these questions has important implications for the Christian life. Theology is not a closed system of established truths but a living, dynamic search for the truth, the partial success of the search only stimulating the desire to reflect more deeply on the inexhaustible riches of Christ. The importance of an attitude of reverence before the incomprehensible reality of the Christian God coupled with the desire to search ever more deeply for the truth of this living God can hardly be exaggerated in the work of preaching and catechizing.

Anyone who has ever undertaken the task knows how difficult it is to teach the Christian religion. What is often obscured is the fact that the difficulty does not lie wholly or even primarily with pedagogy or psychology. I make no claim in this work that a theological understanding of revelation is sufficient to guarantee success in catechetical work. What I do maintain is that such an understanding is an indispensable part of all attempts to improve religious education. It is true that most catechetical writing today reflects the immense wealth of material stemming from biblical and liturgical scholarship. It is also true, however, that a continuing and deeper research on a theological level is necessary if there is to be thorough reform of and lasting improvement in religious education. The theological summaries made in catechetical works usually are not sufficiently detailed for establishing the kind of foundation needed. I have, therefore, devoted this volume to a theological exposition of the nature of revelation. In a book to follow this one I apply the theology of revelation to the field of religious education in order either to support or to challenge some of the catechetical principles being advocated today.[4]

Far from indicating disparagement of psychological or socio-

[4] *Catechesis of Revelation* (New York, Herder and Herder, 1966).

logical studies, this theological study demands for its completion and implementation continuing work in these other areas. While granting the importance of sociological and psychological studies, I nevertheless contend that a great part of our pastoral difficulty lies in our failure to raise in all seriousness the most fundamental question of the nature of revelation. It is to that question that we must now turn.

I.

The Question of Revelation

REVELATION is one of the most basic categories of Christianity. This being true, it might at first seem inexplicable that the nature of revelation has been so little explored by Catholic theologians. Actually, however, it is not so surprising that this should be the case, for the movement from the more immediate to the more ultimate problems (in an ontological sense) is a natural one. No biblical writer felt constrained to give a formal definition of revelation. There is in fact no conceptually unified presentation of revelation in the Bible as a whole. Neither would it be possible to investigate the meaning of revelation solely by studying one or several technical words in the Bible, for the notion is so omnipresent that it cannot be encompassed in this way. These facts are neither shocking nor surprising.

We might compare the notion of revelation in theology to that of "being" in ordinary human understanding and in philosophy as well. That in terms of which everything else is known is thematized for philosophical inquiry only by a few people and only after many other less fundamental questions have been raised.[1] The question of being is not an immediate one, but this is not to say that the investigation of being is

[1] See Albert Dondeyne, *Contemporary European Thought and Christian Faith* (Pittsburgh, Duquesne University, 1958), p. 47.

22

unimportant philosophically. It does mean that metaphysics, coming late upon the scene and finding its object everywhere, can only be a "recollection" of what has always been present to human consciousness though it has been there implicitly or unthematically.

If this analogy is generally valid, we should expect that the Bible, the Church fathers, and the medieval scholastics would tell us little explicitly about the nature of revelation. They do, on the other hand, provide us with much material for reflection, material which includes not only theological teachings but the concrete life of the Church. The Church has often understood aspects of her own nature in a global and unreflexive way, in terms of the lives of her people and the practices of her worship, before she has arrived at a precise conceptual expression of this knowledge. Because revelation is so basic to the Christian religion it is more than a little likely that the Church has already understood much about the nature of revelation at the level of practice which is only now being thematized for theological inquiry. This thematization of revelation was still almost unknown at the beginning of modern times. The basic concern until then seemed to be the analysis and defense of particular dogmas. Only under the pressure of attacks by rationalism, immanentism, and agnosticism did it become clear that the central issue was the possibility and meaning of divine revelation itself.[2]

During this very period of the seventeenth to the twentieth centuries Catholic theologians thought it necessary to emphasize very strongly certain elements of the Catholic faith that had been attacked by Protestants. Though one may doubt that the Council of Trent should be held responsible for all of this emphasis, it is a fact that post-Tridentine Catholic theology

[2] See Roger Aubert, *Le problème de l'acte de foi* (3rd ed.; Louvain, E. Waring, 1958), pp. 680–681.

tended to reserve the term "revelation" for the object of faith as it is presented in propositions.[3] The almost exclusive emphasis upon this aspect of revelation makes it difficult to assert that the vehement criticism of Catholic theology for its depersonalizing, objectifying, and conceptualizing of revelation is entirely groundless. To admit this fact is not to overcome the fault, but the recognition that it is indeed our most fundamental notions which need careful rethinking is the first step toward a deeper understanding of our faith.

Since it is the very notion of revelation that is now challenged and called into question, Catholic theology faces a crisis in its foundations. Such a crisis presents both grave dangers and at the same time great possibilities. "The real 'movement' of the sciences takes place when their basic concepts undergo a more or less radical revision which is transparent to itself. The level which a science has reached is determined by how far it is *capable* of a crisis in its basic concepts."[4]

The theology of revelation that is emerging in response to this crisis is thus clarifying the task of theology itself. Like philosophy, theology is a never ending, radical reflection upon its own first principles, principles which become progressively clearer in the course of time. Theology, as well as philosophy, is an eternal beginning, moving outward from its starting point only far enough to reground its original position. This understanding of theological reflection may seem to make it useless or frustrating. What it should convey, on the contrary, is the optimistic conviction that nothing is ever lost to the Church, that much has already been accomplished, and that a richer understanding lies in the future precisely because of this eternal beginning. "The *Summae* our fathers have constructed are marvelous cathedrals. But their merit is precisely their con-

[3] See Latourelle, *op. cit.*, p. 403.
[4] Martin Heidegger, *Being and Time* (London, SCM Press, 1962), p. 29.

viction that the truth is more beautiful than all that has been said about it."[5]

THE IDEA OF REVELATION IN THE RECENT PAST

The abundance of *De Revelatione* treatises in the nineteenth and early twentieth centuries would seem to give the impression that the nature of revelation has been thoroughly analyzed. The chief concern of these works, however, was the *fact* of revelation and the establishment of this fact as a preamble or preparation for the acceptance of Christian faith. The treatment of revelation, in other words, was not a theological reflection carried out in the light of faith, but an attempt for the most part to show reasonable men the reasonableness of Christianity. It is not my purpose here to attack the legitimacy of such studies. I wish merely to indicate that the large treatises on revelation have astonishingly little to say about revelation itself. A brief, carefully worded definition seemed to suffice.

If we wish to ascertain the recent Catholic teaching on the nature of revelation, it is a relatively easy matter. Prescinding for the moment from the individuals who sought to think through the matter in other categories or at a deeper level, we find the theology manuals of the period remarkably unified in their treatment of revelation. There is almost perfect unanimity among writers of the period that revelation is to be defined as the manifestation of truth by divine speech (*locutio Dei*). That there is a solid foundation for this definition both in the Bible and in patristic and scholastic theology we need not prove here. It is noteworthy, however, that the passage from Heb. 1:1 is the one text of Scripture almost always used to justify the definition. When there is no further development of the definition, revelation is taken to mean the instruction of the rational

---

[5] Emile Mersch, *Theology of the Mystical Body* (St. Louis, B. Herder, 1951), p. 23.

creature in truths which he is incapable of reaching by reason alone. There is one nub of controversy over whether God's speech is to be understood primarily as "teaching" or "testifying."[6] Though the implications of this difference are not without importance, the impression one gets from these works is that the disagreement is not serious. There is no fundamental difference on the meaning of "God's speech."

It is undeniable that this consensus of Catholic theologians on the definition of revelation is not without its truth; but that the definitions were anemic and woefully incomplete is no less deniable. Referring to a standard formulation that "revelation taken strictly and in its proper sense is the divinely produced declaration or manifestation of a thing previously unknown," Léonard goes on to observe that "there is a remarkable thing about such a formula: any Christian tone is imperceptible."[7] This lack of Christian tone is not an oversight or an accident. In what is one of the better studies in the early part of the century, the author expressly states that he is setting aside consideration of Christ so as not to complicate his discussion of revelation.[8] From our vantage point this would appear to be a most unfortunate choice and serious omission. I shall for the present, however, refrain from any further criticism of these treatises on revelation in order to consider their origin and context.

To understand the cast of thought in the late nineteenth and early twentieth centuries we should have to consider it against the background of 1) the currents of philosophical and scientific thought in the nineteenth century together with the Catholic

[6] See N. Iung, "Révélation," in *Dictionnaire de théologie catholique*, t. XIII (Paris, Librairie Letouzey et Ané, 1936), col. 2585.

[7] Augustin Léonard, "Toward a Theology of the Word of God," in *The Word. Readings in Theology*, compiled at the Canisianum (New York, P. J. Kenedy and Sons, 1964), p. 75.

[8] See A. Gardeil, *Le donné révélé et la théologie* (Paris, Librairie Victor Lecoffre, 1910), p. 45.

response of Vatican Council I; 2) the modernist crisis within Catholicism in the early part of this century.

The First Vatican Council did not directly treat of the nature of revelation, but its promulgations concerning both infallibility and faith were not without their effects upon this subject.[9] On the one side, the task of the Church, especially the Petrine office, was conceived of as protecting and preserving divine revelation. The Church through pope and bishops is the authoritative teacher of this revelation. She teaches what has been handed down to her by the apostles through whom all revelation came to the Church. On the other side, in its constitution on faith, Vatican I rightly defended the intellectual character of faith, the signs of credibility, and the constitution of the object of faith in apostolic times.

Taken together these two documents had the effect of stressing the "deposit" left by the apostles and guarded by ecclesiastical authority. "The Holy Spirit was promised to the successors of St. Peter not that they might make known new doctrine by his revelation, but rather, that with his assistance they might religiously guard and faithfully explain the revelation or deposit of faith that was handed down through the apostles." To the question of what one is to believe with Catholic faith the answer of the Council seems clear: "By divine and Catholic faith everything must be believed that is contained in the written word of God or in tradition, and that is proposed by the Church as a divinely revealed object of belief either in a solemn decree or in her ordinary, universal teaching."[10]

These pronouncements of Vatican I touching upon the nature of revelation were surely not intended to be exhaustive. The

[9] For the First Vatican Council's placing of infallibility within the context of revelation, see Hans Küng, *Structures of the Church* (New York, Thomas Nelson and Sons, 1964), pp. 352–373; for the *Constitution on Faith*, see Aubert, *op. cit.*, pp. 132–219.

[10] Translations are from John Clarkson *et al., The Church Teaches* (St. Louis, B. Herder, 1955), p. 101, p. 30.

discussions of the Second Vatican Council confirmed what had become increasingly obvious in recent years, namely, that there is far more to be said about faith and revelation than what the First Vatican Council chose to say. Vatican I defended the "believing that" aspect of faith, writes Bulst, but one must not overlook the fact that this is only the formal side of faith.[11]

It is hardly surprising, however, to find theologians after Vatican I stressing the formal side of faith and the objective side of revelation almost to the exclusion of all other considerations. Such emphases are perhaps unavoidable, but they can cause difficulties when the incompleteness of our understanding is not recognized. For example, it is constantly asserted in Catholic writing, usually with little development or explanation, that revelation closed, ceased, or ended with the apostles. That there are no more truths to be added to the deposit of faith is the explicit teaching of Vatican I.[12] Nevertheless, this is only one aspect of the matter. As the discussions of Vatican II have shown, revelation in its fullness does not consist of a collection of truths.[13] It is therefore at least possible to raise the question of how revelation has "closed" in one (objective) sense and yet in some other sense continues to occur. Indeed, I hope in the course of this work to show that revelation may be viewed as a process which only *begins* in its fullness with apostolic times, a process now extending to all history and never to cease. This is a complex issue which I shall not attempt to develop here

11 Bulst, *op. cit.*, p. 126; see also Gabriel Moran, "Faith as Aim in Religious Education" in *Catholic Educational Review*, LXI (February, 1963), pp. 113–117.

12 D1800, D1836.

13 This is not to deny the truth character of revelation. I shall later deal with the place of holy Scripture and the doctrinal teachings of the Church. The one point I wish to make here is that the Second Vatican Council's constitution does not begin with revelation conceived of as statements of truth, but with revelation as the self-communication of God to man. See *Constitution on Divine Revelation*, Chapter I, Article 2.

but will deal with in chapters three, four, six, and ten. The one point which I do wish to make here is that the work of the Second Vatican Council in this area, as Archbishop Lorenz Jaeger of Paderborn said at the third session, has been to complement and balance the work of Vatican I.[14] This means neither a retraction of the statements of the latter nor an addition of patches to its body of declarations, but rather the provision of a wider context of revelation in order to rethink all the pronouncements of Vatican I.

A deepening and extension of the meaning of revelation might have developed earlier if it had not been for the abortive attempt at the beginning of the century in those doctrines grouped under the name of modernism. Some of the isolated statements of modernists on revelation are not unlike recent statements of Catholic theologians. Care must be exercised, however, lest one condemn all the teachings of modernists as false or condemn all modernistic sounding teaching of the present as heretical. What is decisive here is not the isolated statement but the general theological context and the philosophical presuppositions.

It can hardly be doubted today that modernism was vitiated by its nineteenth-century ancestry in which revelation was conceived of not as a gift from without, but as "the progressive unfolding of the immanent principle of divine life."[15] Though nineteenth-century liberalism was not without its attractive side and certain religious values, the defects inherent in the marriage of history and idealism eventually became apparent in both Catholic and Protestant theology. A rather naïve conception of the relation between religious experience and doctrine made impossible its deepening the Catholic understanding of revela-

14 See "La schéma . . . ," p. 1399.
15 H. D. McDonald, *Theories of Revelation. An Historical Study* (London, George Allen and Unwin, 1963), p. 81.

tion or its synthesizing the objective and subjective, personal and doctrinal, temporal and non-temporal characteristics of revelation.[16]

The modernist movement called forth its condemnation by Pope St. Pius X, who reaffirmed the transcendence and objectivity of revelation because, as Latourelle has remarked, modernism "aimed to replace the notions of supernatural revelation and immutable dogma with a religious development for which the individual or collective consciousness is the sole norm."[17] In the aftermath of this modernist crisis it is perhaps understandable that some of the brilliant germinal ideas on revelation put forward by Moehler, Scheeben, Newman, Blondel, and others did not find their immediate fulfillment. Instead, one finds a great hesitancy in admitting any role to religious experience or to the development of doctrine. It is repeatedly asserted that Christian revelation, having been delivered to the apostles and fixed in unchanging truths, does not depend upon intimate and personal experience, but upon clearly defined concepts and absolute affirmations.[18]

Though progress toward a thorough theological examination of revelation was thus slowed down by the modernist crisis, the winds of change in the twentieth century guaranteed that such an examination would soon come. In the last quarter century and even more in the last five years there has been increasing realization and admission of the fact that the nature of revelation requires profounder investigation. We can consider briefly some of the reasons for the present emergence and clarification of the problem.

[16] See Aubert, *op. cit.,* pp. 368–392; for a philosophical criticism of the modernist position, see A. Marc, "L'idée de révélation," in *Gregorianum,* XXXIV (1953), pp. 390–402.

[17] Latourelle, *op. cit.,* p. 312.

[18] See Gardeil, *op. cit.,* pp. 53–56.

PRESENT INFLUENCES

1. The Scriptural Movement

If we wish to single out the primary factor influencing the development of a deeper understanding of the nature of revelation, the choice would undoubtedly be modern biblical scholarship. After suffering from some hesitation engendered by the times, Catholic exegesis has come fully into its own since the 1943 encyclical of Pope Pius XII, *Divino afflante Spiritu.*

Guardini has written that only revelation can tell us what revelation is; if this be true, biblical study cannot help but play a central role in this enterprise.[19] What the Bible has to say about revelation may have seemed obvious enough to theologians of the past, but the fact is that vast riches have since been discovered in the Bible which were not known, were not even accessible in the past. Both the masters of the thirteenth century and the pioneers of present-day theology were hampered to some degree by the inadequacy of their biblical knowledge.

On the surface the expressions for revelation used in the Bible and in the theological treatises are quite similar. The theology manuals, however, inevitably betray an air of aridity unless they are enriched by more than proof-texts from Scripture. The phrase *"locutio Dei"* that appears in all the theology books need not be eliminated, but it must be seen in the light of the biblical meaning of "word of God" in both Old and New Testaments. What the biblical movement has done, therefore, is to open out the historical, personal, social, and eschatological dimensions of "word of God." These dimensions were far from evident in the theological treatises even though they were not absent from the best of Christian tradition.[20] It is particularly

[19] Guardini, *Offenbarung,* pp. 118–119.

[20] See C. Dumont, "Unité et diversité des signes de la Révélation," in *Nouvelle revue théologique,* LXXX (February, 1958), p. 134; Louis Bouyer, *The Word, Church and Sacraments* (New York, Desclée Co., 1961), p. 19.

important that Christ as the Word transform all subsidiary meanings of the expression, a fact that has not always been sufficiently recognized in theology books.

The development in biblical scholarship met with a development in the theology of the Church, especially the notion of tradition, to bring both the search for and the need for a better grasp of revelation into sharper focus. The somewhat surprising methodology of the definition of the dogma of the Assumption in 1950 raised several theological questions. What had long been apparent to many theologians now became an inescapable fact, that is, that the meaning of tradition was far more complicated than the catechism or manual presentation of it admitted.[21] Theologians were forced to grapple with problems concerning the development of doctrine, the senses of Scripture, and the relation between hierarchy and faithful in the transmission of doctrine.

One of the results of these discussions was the Scripture-tradition controversy of the 1950's. Some Catholic theologians had come to hold that all revelation is contained in holy Scripture at least implicitly. Instead of adding other truths, tradition would occupy a more formal or interpretive role. Other theologians claimed that this opinion was directly opposed to the Church's teaching, especially as formulated by the Council of Trent. In an earlier survey of this question I came to the conclusion that although the controversy was a significant one, it was hampered by a too superficial view of revelation. I then maintained—and it can be even more strongly asserted today—that the question "Is all revelation contained in scripture?" is unanswerable and unintelligible unless there is presupposed a clear understanding of what revelation is and how *any* revelation

21 For the development of the notion of tradition, see Yves Congar, *The Meaning of Tradition* (New York, Hawthorn Books, 1964).

is contained in Scripture or anywhere else.[22] The discussions of Vatican II have confirmed this conclusion. Whereas in the 1962 session the chief point of controversy seemed to be the Scripture-tradition problem, it had become clear by 1964 that the Scripture-tradition question is merely indicative of a much deeper question, the nature of revelation itself.

2. Philosophy

Although theological studies on revelation must rely most heavily upon the Bible, human reflection in the form of philosophy necessarily commands a significant role. Every attempt to escape the use of philosophy in considering revelation falls prey to the hidden and unexamined ingestion of philosophical concepts and presuppositions. While some branches of Protestantism have attempted to avoid this conclusion, the Catholic tradition has always maintained it rather strongly. In attempting to relate philosophy to this subject, however, there are two dangers to be avoided. On the one hand, the general philosophical climate may be so opposed to Christian revelation that it threatens to destroy it. At other times, the reverse is true, that is, philosophy seems so closely allied to revelation that there is danger that it may absorb it.

The paradox of the contemporary philosophical scene is the presence of both of these dangers at one and the same time. Although the intervention of a transcendent God bestowing a supernatural revelation is antithetical to much of contemporary thought, one yet finds in modern philosophy many of the same themes with which biblical theology is concerned. Many of the most influential philosophers of the century are not Christians and yet they have influenced or have been influenced by the religious movements within Christianity. The student of the

[22] See Gabriel Moran, *Scripture and Tradition* (New York, Herder and Herder, 1963), and also: "Scripture-Tradition: Witness to Revelation," in *Continuum,* I (Autumn, 1963), pp. 343–354.

Bible will find himself on ground not entirely unfamiliar when he meets the body-subject in Merleau-Ponty, encounter in Buber, truth as unveiling in Heidegger, freedom in Sartre, or transcendence in Jaspers. Whether or not and to what extent any of these philosophical notions are in fact helpful for developing an understanding of Christian revelation is a matter that demands careful consideration.

The one point that I wish to make here is that the development of a theology of revelation has been hastened by the break up and at the same time enrichment of philosophical thought among Catholic theologians. A period of rather narrowly conceived neo-scholasticism seems definitely a thing of the past. The phenomenology of language and symbolism, the currents of personalist and existentialist thought, the study of history and cosmic evolution are all contributing to a synthesis of theology of revelation.

Especially in twentieth-century philosophy is the "re-grounding" of metaphysics by Martin Heidegger of great significance here. Within the Catholic tradition and more immediately related to our subject, the ontology of knowledge in the work of Joseph Maréchal and Karl Rahner would seem to be of incalculable importance for a theology of revelation.[23] The metaphysical inquiries have in turn given birth to new epistemological study at a deeper level than that possible in recent centuries. Questions of faith and revelation can no longer be considered peripheral or insignificant even by philosophers who are not believers.

3. Ecumenism

Except for the period of modernist crisis, Catholic theological concerns seemed curiously remote from the currents affecting

[23] Joseph Maréchal, *Le point de départ de la metaphysique,* Cahier V (2nd ed.; Paris, Desclée de Brouwer, 1949); and Karl Rahner, *Geist in Welt* (2nd ed.; München, Kösel, 1957).

34

Protestantism in the late nineteenth and early twentieth centuries. In recent years this state of affairs has changed dramatically. First by reason of common scriptural research and now through broader ecumenical interest, the era of unconcern has passed. With the increased mutual interest and communication, Catholic students and scholars have discovered a large body of Protestant literature on the theology of revelation. Since Barth's attacks upon liberalism a half century ago, numerous Protestant theologians have written treatises on the nature of revelation. These writings are so rich and variegated that no summary of them will be attempted within this work. But if I may hazard one generalization about this twentieth-century Protestant writing, it would be that it has rejected anything resembling a "propositional notion" of revelation. Action, event, and encounter are words to be met everywhere; knowledge, truth, and revealed doctrine are admitted if at all only as secondary in revelation.[24]

Catholic theologians, instead of reacting with defensive polemics, have to a large extent been carefully examining what Protestant writers have to say on this subject. At times the Protestant notions are found to be incompatible with Catholicism. Very often, however, if Protestant writing on revelation does not furnish Catholic theology with answers, it does open up areas of research and force Catholic theologians to raise some of the same questions. Even a writer such as Rudolf Bultmann, whose work on revelation would seem to set him directly at odds with Catholic doctrine, has been given a serious and sympathetic hearing by many Catholic theologians.[25] Whatever direction

[24] See John Baillie, *The Idea of Revelation in Recent Thought* (New York, Columbia University, 1956); Walter Horton, "Revelation," in *A Handbook of Christian Theology*, edited by M. Halverson (New York, Meridian Books, 1958), p. 327.

[25] See Louis Malevez, *The Christian Message and Myth* (Westminster, Newman, 1957); Joseph Cahill, "Rudolf Bultmann's Concept of Revelation," in *Catholic Biblical Quarterly*, XXIV (July, 1962), pp. 297–306.

35

Protestant writing may take in the near future, it has now raised questions which simply will not go away, and both Catholic and Protestant theology must face up to these ultimate issues.[26]

4. The Catechetical Movement

I said in my Introduction that a theology of revelation should be of great significance for the current attempts to improve preaching and catechizing. The converse relationship is also true; that is, the pastoral movements of recent years have been a main impetus in the development of a theology of revelation.

In 1936 Josef Jungmann published his work, *The Good News and Our Proclamation of the Faith,* which decried the lack of understanding of faith on the part of many Catholics. Jungmann called for a renewal of preaching and catechizing by bringing their content more into line with Scripture and liturgy. Thus there began the so-called "kerygmatic theology" movement which continued for more than a decade in European circles.[27] The desire of the "kerygmatists" was clear: they wanted a pastoral renewal which would overcome the aridity and ineffectiveness of current approaches.[28] How precisely to accomplish this pastoral renewal was not so easy to say.

The solution which Jungmann seemed to indicate was to leave dogmatic theology as it was and set up a parallel theology which would be strongly scriptural, non-philosophical, and

[26] See Raymond Brown, "After Bultmann What? An Introduction to the Post-Bultmannians," in *Catholic Biblical Quarterly,* XXVI (January, 1964), pp. 1–30.

[27] See Emil Kappler, *Die Verkündigungstheologie* (Freiburg, Schweiz, Paulusverlag, 1949), pp. 1–110; Domenico Grasso, "The Good News and the Renewal of Theology," in Josef Jungmann, *The Good News Yesterday and Today* (New York, Sadlier, 1962), pp. 201–211.

[28] See Andrés A. Esteban Romero, "La controversia en torno a la teología kerigmática," in *XV Semana Española de Teología* (Madrid, 1956), p. 371.

directly pastoral.[29] Although this vision was tempting and some people did strive to create a purely "kerygmatic theology," such a solution could not be the final one. This solution, as Urs von Balthasar has asserted, "if carried to its conclusion, would mean perpetuating the mischievous cleavage in theology, and would be tantamount to declaring bankrupt the speculative power of reason enlightened by faith."[30] Theologians who opposed the establishment of a separate theology had to admit the aridity of much modern theology, but they claimed that theology need not be that way. They were thus forced to reflect upon their science's foundation and methods and to ask whether theology was coming to grips with the central questions of Christian revelation.

There gradually emerged from this controversy the clear conviction that theology cannot be pastoral unless it is true to itself, that is, deeply biblical, thoroughly scientific, and intensely concerned with the central issues of revelation. The task of modern theology then became obvious: to return to the deepest sources of theology's power, to enrich theology with the best of human reflection, and to bring theology into a dynamic unity that would take account of the personal, historical, and social. Within that context theologians must ask themselves daily, as it were, the basic question we pose here: What is revelation?

[29] Jungmann later denied that he was proposing a new kind of theology; see Josef Jungmann, "Theology and Kerygmatic Teaching," in *Lumen Vitae,* V (April, 1950), p. 263: "We do not, however, intend to set up a new theology against dogmatic theology. The discussion which was started some ten years ago in many German and a few foreign reviews on the need for a kerygmatic theology has been side-tracked and has got far away from the real question. The main point is not that of an independent theology, but that of special rules for preaching in the light of theology."

[30] Hans Urs von Balthasar, *Word and Redemption* (New York, Herder and Herder, 1965), p. 66.

II.

Revelation and History

IN contemporary theological writing, both Catholic and Protestant, there are few points more consistently emphasized than that of the historical character of Christian revelation. It is repeatedly said that in the Christian view of things history is not merely preliminary to revelation but is revelation itself. The special character of biblical revelation is that God has revealed himself in historical events.[1]

It is impossible to trace here the "history of salvation" in the manner of today's textbooks; nor can I deal with the numerous historical problems connected with the study of the Bible. I wish rather to raise the question of the essential relation between history and revelation. I say "raise the question" because this relationship is of such complexity and has been the subject of such debate that I make no pretense of solving the whole matter here. I intend in this chapter, however, to establish a few principles concerning revelation and history that will lead to the posing of a dilemma at the end of this chapter. From there the following chapters will several times return to this problem of history in trying to work toward a resolution of this problem.

---

[1] See Edmond Jacob, *Theology of the Old Testament* (New York, Harper and Brothers, 1958), p. 188; Bruce Vawter, "The Historical Theology of the Gospels," in *Homiletic and Pastoral Review*, LXII (May, 1962), p. 685.

At first sight the constantly repeated assertion that revelation does not consist in propositional truths but in historical saving actions of God seems straightforward and unambiguous. It is true, of course, that until very recently Catholic works did not present revelation as a "salvation history," but the conviction of its historical nature is now taken as almost axiomatic in scriptural, theological, catechetical, and liturgical writing. It would be difficult to find anyone who is completely opposed to this trend in the presentation of revelation. Some people, however, may have the uneasy feeling that history is simply being used as a new category into which revelation is placed while there is yet no deeper penetration into the nature of revelation itself.

At least one Protestant theologian, James Barr, has hit out strongly at contemporary theology's assumptions concerning revelation and history. He writes, "Revelation through history is, to use Galbraith's term, the conventional wisdom of modern theology. Historians of theology in a future age will look back on the mid-twentieth century and call it the revelation-in-history period."[2] Barr goes on to charge that history is in fact a nonbiblical category, that history cannot be normative for biblical study since substantial parts of the Old Testament do not come under this motif, that contrary to claims made today a "history of salvation" means very little to twentieth-century man. "There is then a real danger," he continues, "that revelation through history may furnish us with reasonably good apologetic in relation to the questions raised in the nineteenth century, but not in relation to those which are likely to arise in the later twentieth."[3]

Even if one disagrees with Barr's contentions, one is forced by his remarks to examine more deeply what is meant by a

[2] James Barr, "Revelation through History in the Old Testament and in Modern Theology," in *New Theology No. 1*, edited by Martin E. Marty and Dean G. Peerman (New York, Macmillan, 1964), pp. 61–62.
[3] *Ibid.*, p. 71.

revelation through history. When it is so often insisted upon that revelation must be understood as history, there is seldom advertence to the fact that the meaning of the word "history" may itself not be clear. Because of the ambiguity of the word "history," some rather startling paradoxes arise. Christian theologians, for example, often give all the credit to the Jews for founding history, while among modern historiographers, any Jewish contribution is often dismissed as insignificant. Among most moderns, it is Thucydides and Herodotus, not Moses and Solomon, who are credited with being our early historians. On the one hand, we read that the Jews had a keen historical sense and that it was precisely their historical understanding that differentiated them from other ancient peoples. On the other hand, it is also said that "if by history is meant knowledge of the past, it is fair to recognize with L. Koehler that the Hebrew mind had little awareness of the notion of history, for it is interested in history only to the extent in which it is *hic et nunc* a present and dynamic reality."[4]

Exegetes have wrestled with this problem of the historical in their consideration of literary forms; but such discussion needs to be placed against the background of the whole revelational process. Ultimately, it was not the choice of the biblical writer to "distort the facts." The nature of the material was the main reason for the kind of writing that emerged from the biblical writers. This "material" was God's dealing with man in the events of man's own personal life. The biblical writers were convinced that what was primary was not some pattern of impersonal events and message, but God and man's relation to God.

The Jews of the Old Testament, therefore, were not particularly interested in the amassing of precise details to be recorded as objectively as possible. They would thus be lacking one of the fundamental requirements for those who engage in

[4] Jacob, *op. cit.,* p. 184.

40

modern historical research. The belief of the Jews, however, did lead them to make what in one sense was a small and yet in another sense a crucial contribution to the growth of historical study: they took man's life seriously. They accepted the thoroughly temporal character of human life believing that the human temporal events possessed a depth of meaning. In light of this it would appear that it was precisely the rejection of the temporal happening as primary locus of meaning that vitiated Greek historical writing after an auspicious start.[5]

We might conclude, therefore, that though they did not undertake a scientific study of the past, the Jews did make a valuable contribution to historical study. A positivistic theory of history would not be able to admit the importance of their contribution, but twentieth-century historiography has largely moved away from the positivistic. There is today more of a realization that history must not be viewed as a process of events or a collection of facts into which man is fitted, but that history is man's own life of self-understanding.[6] What we have said so far should indicate that we must be attentive to man's self-understanding before God. Appreciating an historical revelation will mean investigating more closely the process of interrelationship of God and the Jewish people.

THE JEWISH EXPERIENCE OF GOD

In our attempt to understand what is distinctive of Jewish religious experience, we might begin by noting that it was not national genius that was the foundation of Old Testament reve-

[5] See Karl Löwith, *Meaning in History* (Chicago, Phoenix Books, 1949), pp. 185–186; Rudolph Bultmann, *The Presence of Eternity* (New York, Harper and Brothers, 1957), pp. 14–22; Eric Voegelin, *Order and History*, vol. I: *Israel and Revelation* (Baton Rouge, Louisiana State University, 1956), pp. 116–133.

[6] See R. G. Collingwood, *The Idea of History* (Oxford, Clarendon Press, 1946), pp. 282–315; Friedrich Gogarten, *Demythologizing and History* (London, SCM Press, 1955), pp. 12–33; Alan Richardson, *History Sacred and Profane* (Philadelphia, Westminster, 1964), pp. 154–183.

lation. "The revelation and the belief of the Old Testament are not 'Jewish religion,'" as Guardini has remarked, "but instead realize themselves in a struggle against the natural religious self-assertions of the people."[7] The Old Testament was based upon a presupposition distinct from the religious character of a people. It was based upon the belief that God had chosen to enter into a personal relationship with man and that he therefore communicated with a particular group of people in a particular place and in a determined time. In what way this distinguishes Old Testament revelation from other supposed revelations can be seen by analyzing each of these characteristics separately and then bringing them together in the notion of "word."

1.

God entered the life of man in the real experience which man has of his temporal existence. There is a sense in which all religions have a revelation and even a revelation in time, but the time in non-Jewish religions was a mythical time, a transcendent instant in the beginning. This is the Gnostic tendency "dominated by the nostalgia for an initial situation which commands all actuality by a myth of the *Urzeit* and *Ursprung*."[8] For the Jews, on the contrary, the continuing temporal situation had real meaning and religious value. Time had this meaning because God who transcends and dominates time had chosen to enter time and to be graciously present within time. This belief in God's communication in the temporal situations of man's life implied an anthropology. Man in his entire temporal mode of existence is the one who is related to God. It is not an

[7] Guardini, *Offenbarung*, p. 57.

[8] Henri-Charles Puech, "Gnosis and Time," in *Man and Time. Papers from the Eranos Yearbooks* (New York, Pantheon, 1957), p. 82.

atemporal spark of the divine that must answer to God, but man the temporal being who must answer. There had always been time in man's existence but because time means change and change means decay and death, time was too frightening to face. It was only through faith in the one who gave meaning to time that man was given the capacity to face his real, temporal life.[9]

2.

What has been said of time is similarly true of place. For God to be present to men at a particular time meant, too, a presence in one place. To know God was to recognize that he was present within a situation, that he was there among his people. He was in one place not because he was confined by spatial qualities, but because while mastering all space he had graciously bestowed his presence to individuals who exist only within the limitations of space. He was at once the King of Israel in a special sense and the Lord of the universe, before whom any other gods were as nothing.

3.

In order to establish a personal relationship with man, God elected certain people, chosen ones who experienced his presence in a special way. God's gift of himself to the charismatic, however, was not for the benefit of the isolated individual. The choice was not so much a privilege as it was a responsibility to serve. God met the individual within Israel and Israel herself in the real-life situations in which they were related to other men. It was not a non-social side of man that was addressed by God,

[9] See Mircea Elieade, *Cosmos and History* (New York, Harper Torchbook, 1959), pp. 139–162; Eric Frank, *Philosophical Understanding and Religious Truth* (New York, Oxford, 1945), pp. 67–73.

but man constituted by the social relations which structure his existence.[10]

4.

We may bring together these dimensions of Old Testament revelation under the image most often used in the Bible itself: God spoke a *word*. Exegetes in recent years have tried to bring out the wealth of meaning in the biblical term "word."[11] There is some difficulty in accomplishing this task. The biblical "word" has a richness of meaning which does not fit our concept because there is a different way of thinking that underlies the use of the concepts and words.

For our purposes we may say that God's word is expressive of the power and call of God directed to man, the spatio-temporal and social being. The "word" is that which is spoken by a person to a person; it is an invitation to some kind of personal interrelationship. What was primary in this conception was not something spoken or written, but God's self bestowal in space, time, and community calling to man's freedom.

Because God was taking to himself man, then his loving invitation was expressed through a multiplicity of human symbols, that is, words, actions, attitudes, gestures that are expressive of man. Foremost among these symbols is the human word, and so it was especially in human words that the divine power shone forth. God took hold of men who claimed that they were not speaking on their own but were speaking the word of God. (See Jer. 20:9; Amos 3:8.) Yet insofar as it was a word spoken by man, in one human language, in one social context, it was a truly human word with the limitations of human language. Even

[10] See Guardini, *Offenbarung*, p. 61.
[11] See John L. McKenzie, "The Word of God in the Old Testament," in *Theological Studies*, XXI (June, 1960), pp. 183–206.

had God dictated the words, they would have been human words mediating the divine call.[12]

God's meeting with man in his concrete, bodily, social existence thus issued in human words; these words emerged in spoken and written forms so as to take on an existence of their own. Though such a process is both necessary and inevitable, the danger always is that the origin and meaning of "word of God" will be obscured. Words separated from personal relationships eventually become stagnant and empty. In no case is this danger so serious as in the words which are meant to mediate the relation of divine and human. The regrounding of conceived, spoken, and written words cannot take place only by reference to the occasion of the speaking; there must be reference to the one who speaks. In God's revelation the union of activity and interpretive word will always break down or will be kept together artificially unless it is always realized that the most important question is neither event nor word but God.

"The quintessence of divine revelation in the Old Testament," writes Schillebeeckx, "is expressed in several places thus: 'I will be your God, and you will be my people.' "[13] (See Ex. 6:7, Lev. 26:12, etc.) Historical events are of great significance but their significance derives from the people (God and men) who are ultimate. If we speak of revelation as historical events, this can only mean events in the life of a human subject who takes part in and to some degree consciously grasps the meaning of these events as relating him to God. There is an inescapable tendency to reduce revelation to things or objects. But to place revelation

[12] Not only the prophetic saying but also the law in Israel was regarded as God's word; see T. C. Vriezen, *An Outline of Old Testament Theology* (Oxford, Blackwell, 1960), p. 256: "Fundamentally *torah* in the Old Testament denotes God's *revelational decision* and points to guidance that God would give His people in their everyday life through the intermediary of the official representatives of the people. A translation of *torah* by 'word of revelation' would come closer to the original meaning."

[13] Edward Schillebeeckx, *Christ the Sacrament of the Encounter with God* (New York, Sheed and Ward, 1963), p. 12.

45

outside man, whether in a book, in an institution, or in a schema of historical reports, can only result in depersonalizing revelation and exhausting it of its central significance.

I do not mean to deny that there are objective realities in the revelational process. Precisely because God's revelation was to man there had to be objective elements. I have pointed out that in the Jewish revelation there was express correlation to time, place, and communal structure. I do insist, however, that these are elements in man's history and that they are revelatory only through their relation to the human subject. The term of God's revelatory activity is always man, the being who can consciously and freely respond to God's love.

Revelation as a Continuing Process

God's activity with man cannot be conceived of as a series of isolated events each accompanied by a word of interpretation. If it is man's whole self that is in question, there must be an organic process in which the words issue out of life and point back to what is non-verbal in life.[14] The early experiences of the Jewish people were already communicative of great meaning to those attentive to the presence and demands of God. To be a fully personal relationship, however, human words had to be spoken to draw out the implicit meaning of these experiences. Words bring meaning to light by interpreting what has been given in experience; there is not full intelligibility until such interpretive words are spoken.[15] It is not surprising, therefore, that in God's dealing with Israel the continuing experience of God's activity raised up men who spoke interpretive words after having reflected deeply upon their own lives and those of their brothers. These men were the prophets.

[14] See *Constitution on Divine Revelation*, Chapter I, Article 2.
[15] See: G. E. Wright, *God Who Acts* (Chicago, Henry Regnery Co., 1952), p. 84.

The prophet is not one who has concepts and truths infused into him by God. He is rather the one who with his spirit, his heart, and his entire life reflects upon the experience of his people. Thereby he brings to light the meaning of events, persons, visions, ecstasies, images, dreams. Prophecy is not something which drops down from heaven to violate the natural order of things. It is, if we may use the expression, the natural result in a history in which God takes part. Prophecy is not revelation, but revelation emerges in prophecy as the meaning of words appears in the words or as the person expresses himself in bodily symbol.[16]

Prophecy is not only the effect of revelation. Within the continuing intercourse of God and man, prophecy is the cause of a clearer revelation, just as all verbal expression brings to fulfillment the experience which causes it while at the same time it effects a deepening of the original experience. Human discourse is always a process of active response in which each word is both cause and effect within the continuing conversation. Prophecy, therefore, is not the passive, inert reception of something. It is the active human response that the prophet makes in the light of his reflection (directed by a divine charism) to his own experience and that of the nation.

The prophetic understanding is directed not to isolated actions but to human life in its full temporality. Because man is not only temporal but also knows that he is temporal, the acceptance of his real-life situation will always involve a synthesizing of his past, present, and future. Every human statement bears some reference to past, present, and future; a fortiori is this true of every prophetic statement. "A present experience is true and valuable only insofar as it is bound up with a certain vision and interpretation of the past and future, with a projec-

[16] See Pierre Benoit, "Révélation et Inspiration," in Revue biblique, LXX (1963), p. 370; Dennis McCarthy, "Personality, Society and Inspiration," in Theological Studies, XXIV (December, 1963), p. 572.

tion of our ruling ideal, in the memory that guides us. The Bible is filled with such projections toward its own historic past. Without them it would not possess a truth that was fully human."[17]

The prophets of Israel, therefore, could not avoid references to the past. Their interpretation of present experience was in terms of and in the symbolism of the great themes of election and covenant. At the same time, they could not help but project an image into the future though the concrete realization of what they affirmed for the future was beyond their comprehension. This imagery of past and future should not mislead us; the prophets are men who live in the present and whose chief concern is the God who is now revealing himself, now addressing man. The question they "raise in every critical moment is about the interpretation of what is going on, whether what is happening be, immediately considered, a drought or the invasion of a foreign army, or the fall of a great empire. Israel is the people that is to see and understand the action of God in everything that happens and to make a fitting reply."[18]

The prophetic understanding does not do away with the need for reason, experience, and memory. But beginning with the nucleus of insight into the present moment, the light of prophecy illuminates the rest of experience by casting the light of intelligibility upon it. The scattered happenings of the past were thus brought together in an intelligible whole. When the Old Testament emerged from the Jewish people it was not so much a recording of "revelations" as it was the history of the Jewish people unified and understood through the prophetic understanding.[19]

[17] Han Urs von Balthasar, "God Speaks as Man," in *Word and Revelation* (New York, Herder and Herder, 1964), p. 96.

[18] H. Richard Niebuhr, *The Responsible Self* (New York, Harper and Row, 1963), p. 67.

[19] See Richardson, *History Sacred and Profane*, p. 224; Voegelin, *Israel and Revelation*, pp. 134–144.

In the human situation the interpretation of events and the conveyance of meaning take place within a context that is generally larger than we realize, and is in fact indefinitely extensible. Prophetic interpretation was a continuous reinterpretation from an ever widening context of understanding. The reinterpreted meaning was constantly being taken up into the revelational process. God's designs for mankind could not have been delivered to prophets in the form of truths to be enunciated. There simply were no self-contained statements that could convey in an even relatively adequate way what God intended for man.

God began the dialogue at the level at which man was to be found. God's invitation to a higher life consisted first of all in the actions of love and kindness which could enable man to recognize himself as lovable and give him the courage to face his own condition. Every act of love on God's part, every response on man's part, changed the revelatory position of man *vis-à-vis* God. As man came to accept his own self, entrusting himself to his partner in dialogue, the reality of God became clearer and at the same time his own destiny came into view more clearly.[20] Every recognized and accepted act of God's love for him threw light upon his past and opened possibilities for the future, so that saved from the torturing anxieties of past faults and future uncertainties he could become more truly present to himself, to his neighbor, and to God.

What is true of all free, personal relationships is preëminently true of the relation of God and man. There is the possibility that despite a successful start one partner may refuse to give and may turn in upon himself and away from the other. From the first moment of their dialogue God knew the weakness of man. He knew that despite all his testimonies of love and fidelity man would draw back and prefer to take a path that seemed easier. An education of man to faith and freedom could not help but

[20] See Hans Urs von Balthasar, *A Theology of History* (New York, Sheed and Ward, 1963), p. 120.

be a slow, halting, painful process in which God and man became "accustomed" to one another.[21]

Every time that man said "no," God's "yes" remained firm. Not that God's affirmation overran man's freedom, but God found a new starting point and a new route along which to travel in the dialogue with man. God had thus bound himself to the limitations of his partner; he had made himself weak to save the weak. The most amazing thing about revelation, it would seem, is that the sins of men not only did not break off the relation, but in a certain sense became part of the revelational process. "Man's fall ought not to occur," Guardini has said; "yet after it has happened, it becomes the presupposition for a new revelation."[22] Man's rebellion and fall simply became the occasion for new revelatory action on God's part. Unlike a human partner whose love and patience are finite, God refused to leave man to the selfishness that would eventually destroy him. God knew that he must gently draw man forward, not simply by disregarding his failures, but by using even failure to bring man to see what man is and what God is.

These considerations lead us to conclude that revelation in its most basic sense is neither a word coming down from heaven to which man assents nor an historical event manifesting a truth. It would be better to begin by conceiving of revelation as an historical and continuing intersubjective communion in which man's answer is part of the revelation. "We are now able to discern in the texts the Jews' much more profound, more existential participation in the very substance of the word of God so much so in fact that the word of revelation simply cannot be separated from the articulate human response like kernel from husks."[23] If faith and revelation are to be personal then

21 On this point, as developed by St. Irenaeus, see Jean Daniélou, *Christ and Us* (New York, Sheed and Ward, 1961), pp. 94–101.

22 Guardini, *Offenbarung*, p. 60.

23 Hans Urs von Balthasar, *Martin Buber and Christianity* (New York, Macmillan, 1962), p. 21.

50

there must be a true interpersonal reality which is not merely the juxtaposing of subjective and objective elements. Unless one considers in all seriousness the human person who is himself within the revelation and not outside it, all attempts to unite "revealed truths" with "revelatory events" will be unsuccessful.

The Old Testament revelation as an interpersonal communion of free individuals moved forward according to the rhythm inherent in human life. At a later stage there was truth and meaning in experience which simply was not there previously. Reading "truths" into the earlier parts of the Old Testament that could not have been known and expressed at that point of time does violence both to the sacred text and to the authenticity of the divine-human relationship.[24] On the other hand, we are not prevented from seeing more in the text than he who uttered it was directly aware of. Given the continuing historical process we have described, every human affirmation contained a significance which the human person asserting it could not have been conscious of. Since each subsequent action threw light upon man's past and his future, the ultimate meaning of every event and word within the process could be judged only from beyond the process. The unity and intelligibility of the whole process could be seen only from the unity of intention of the person whose acts in history constituted a unified plan. The final unity of the Old Testament is not found in the Old Testament, but only in its completion in and conjunction with the New Testament.[25]

As the Old Testament progressed toward its climax, "it was still not apparent how God was going at last to respond to the human answer, usually negative, of his own initiating act: whether the ultimate utterance of the creative Word would be

[24] See Vriezen, *op. cit.*, pp. 52–53; R. M. Grant, *The Letter and the Spirit* (New York, Macmillan, 1957), p. 107.
[25] See *Constitution on Divine Revelation,* Chapter IV, Article 15.

the word of wrath or of love."[26] Though what the end would be seemed still to be in doubt, that there would be an end point, a climax to the process, became unmistakably clear. The conception of history as a personal dialogue meant that the process could only lead either to deeper communion or to final estrangement. Pagan and Greek conceptions of time generally tended to be cyclical in character. Old Testament revelation excluded a cycle of eternal return not because the revelation teaches something different, but because revelation is something different.[27]

Implicit from the beginning in this conception of a linear directed history was the conviction that it was not only Israel that moved toward an end point. The Israelite covenant was paradigmatic for all history. The Lord who established this history was the Lord of all history. The light of intelligibility that had been cast upon Israelite history extended itself beyond her borders. Thus there emerged in the later part of the Old Testament (especially in Daniel, 2 Isaiah) a philosophy of universal history. God, it was believed, will reveal himself in his glory. This will be the end of the revelational process and thereby of history. He will be the Lord of all nations and all peoples.

THE SCANDAL OF HISTORY

This pattern of Old Testament history could be worked out in much greater detail. Instead of doing that, however, I would like to pose the more basic question of the validity, meaning, and relevancy of the whole process. For many of our contem-

[26] Karl Rahner, "Development of Dogma," in *Theological Investigations,* vol. I (Baltimore, Helicon, 1961), p. 49.

[27] See Puech, *loc. cit.,* pp. 42–48; a sharp contrast between Hebrew and Greek concepts of time was expounded by Oscar Cullmann in *Christ and Time* (Philadelphia, Westminster, 1950); this has been criticized by James Barr, *Biblical Words for Time* (Naperville, Ill., Allenson, 1962), pp. 137–140. Even with Barr's criticism, however, the point we make here remains generally valid.

poraries, what is most difficult to accept about Judaic-Christian revelation is not this or that historical detail, but the fact that this revelation is bound to history at all; or more precisely, that this revelation is bound to the history of people at one place at one time in the past. This is what constitutes the "scandal of history" or "scandal of particularity."[28] Some Christians may rejoice in the scandal, and it may be that this is part of that scandal of the cross of which Paul spoke. It is a fact that no one can see the true significance of Israel's history nor the unsurpassable uniqueness of the man of Nazareth without a faith that triumphs over the blindness of flesh.

We must, nevertheless, not attribute incomprehensibility to this central aspect of Christian revelation without careful consideration. The inability of many persons to accept an historical revelation may be due at least in part not to their lack of faith, but to our lack of understanding. The undeniable fact here is that while the historical pattern of Jewish history supplies the theologian and exegete with unity and intelligibility, it is precisely that very pattern which constitutes a grave difficulty today for many people, not all of whom are enemies of Christianity.[29]

It is a most remarkable contention in much theological and catechetical writing today that revelation will become relevant to men's lives if only they will study the history of Israel and realize that God revealed himself in the events of Israelite history. It is founded on the belief that revelation does not consist in "mere intellectual knowledge," but is tied to historical events. But on the other hand, it is this very belief that is for many people at best irrelevant and at worst an insuperable obstacle to accepting this revelation. H. Richard Niebuhr has written, "Concentration on history in the Church has led to repeated

[28] See C. H. Dodd, *The Apostolic Preaching and Its Development* (3rd ed.; London, Hodder and Stoughton, 1963), p. 88.

[29] John Macquarrie, *Twentieth Century Religious Thought* (New York, Harper and Row, 1963), p. 328.

53

revolts by men of piety and good will for whom God was not a 'then and there' but a 'here and now' and for whom faith was not belief in the actuality of historical events but confidence in an abiding, ruling will of love."[30]

This is the crux of the problem which Catholic theology must now face in its insistence upon the historical character of revelation. One of the main points of this chapter has been to indicate that revelation as history means a history in which the individual, as related to the community, himself participates. Thus revelation in my life must mean the events which help to constitute my existence, events which I share in with another who is present to me and opens his life to me. If this is true, it raises the question in what sense a past revelation can still exist. The events of Jewish history may have been revelational to the Jews, but it is precisely the character of historical events to be unrepeatable. The past event may have been recorded and the record passed down, but an event in which one participates and a story about an event in someone else's past are quite different things. In the latter case, one does not have the revelatory event but propositions about the event.

Catholic writers who hope to overcome the abstractedness of faith by introducing historical events as the basis of God's revelation must realize, however, that past events *are* abstractions and conceptualizations, even though we imaginatively describe them and interconnect them. The talk of a personal presentation of revelation as "salvation history" has not greatly impressed anyone outside of a rather narrow circle, because the rooting of man's life in past events not only does not restore value to human history, but, on the contrary, seems to be the most direct denial of it. In a world in which history and progress are highly valued, Catholicism is thus faced with the reproach:

[30] *The Meaning of Revelation* (New York, Macmillan Paperback, 1962), p. 56.

54

"Faith in God destroys in us the sense of historicity and produces fixity of thought and death of consciousness."[31]

Exegetes and theologians stressing the event-character of revelation must face the problem which Bultmann poses:

> Can we speak of the call of God as an event of the past, or rather only as it is God's call directed to me in my situation. . . . If God's word is event, it can be such only to the extent that it is occurring *in actu*. It cannot be event in the sense of a verifiable fact lying in the past. God's revelation [*Offenbarung*] is not publication [*Offenbartheit*].[32]

Non-Catholic theologians have an answer to this problem if they posit a continuing revelation. Catholic doctrine, on the other hand, with its insistence upon the closing of revelation, seems committed to the past over the present and exposed to the charge of not taking history seriously.

When the Catholic doctrine of the closing of revelation is asserted it is usually joined with the statement that the call of God does not cease and that revelation remains in its efficacy and truth. Undoubtedly there is a transcendence of truth, a communicability of understanding from one generation to another. This is so in the philosophical order; it is equally true of the teachings of the prophets and Jesus Christ and of our knowledge of many events in the past.[33] But this is precisely the conception of revelation which Catholic theology is trying to escape from, that is, a revelation that is a collection of truths, teachings, and historical facts.

We are therefore faced with this dilemma: Either revelation is constituted by events in the experience of men in the past and is no longer with us because their experience has ceased;

---

[31] This is the formulation of the objection against the Christian as "reactionary and conservative by vocation" in an article by R. Aubert, as cited in Latourelle, *op. cit.*, p. 380.

[32] As quoted in Vawter, "Historical Theology . . . ," *loc. cit.*, p. 687.

[33] See Bernard Lonergan, *Insight* (Longmans, Green and Co., 1957), p. 707.

or revelation consists of truths not irrevocably tied to temporal events but communicable through propositions from one generation to another. The first of these positions would, of course, be directly opposed to the nature of the Church which claims to be protector and teacher of a revelation, one which has a knowledge and truth character. The latter position is what is opposed in Catholic as well as non-Catholic writing today because it reduces faith to the acceptance of propositional truths coming to man from without. When the protests against a revelation of "mere truths" has been heard the question remains: How can revelation be anything other than truths or objects if it is handed down from one generation to another; or, reversing the question, how can a revelation consisting of personal events in the past ever be a present revelation? The answers given to this problem generally do no more than restate the question or avoid the question with ambiguous language. Phrases such as "liturgy is salvation history here and now" are part of the question and not the answer.

The solution to this difficulty we do not find in the Old Testament. Neither would we find an answer in the New Testament if we were to see it only as a record of more and still greater works on God's part. The key to a personal revelation in the twentieth century lies in the emergence of a human consciousness that is entirely receptive to God revealing and that remains among men to continue that revelation. It is to that person that we now turn.

III.

Christ as Revelatory Communion

AT the third session of Vatican II, in a speech based upon many years of missionary experience, Archbishop (now Cardinal) Paul Zoungrana of the Upper Volta besought the bishops of the Council: "Say to the world that Jesus Christ is the revelation of God so that the figure of Christ may shine forth over the earth."[1] Like many other pastoral pleas at the Council, the remark reflected a significant change in theological emphasis.

In striking contrast to the treatises *De Revelatione* that we mentioned earlier, the person of Jesus Christ has assumed a dominant role in discussions on revelation. Of course, Catholic theology always did give Christ a central place in the deliverance of revelation to mankind; but the statement now almost commonplace in theological writing is that Jesus Christ did not just bring the revelation but that he *is* the revelation. One can hardly deny that there had earlier been a failure to manifest a true Christocentrism in analyses of revelation, a failure which was puzzling if not scandalous to many Protestant brethren. Fortunately, the centrality of the person of Christ in the revelational-redemptive process has now been insisted upon by the Second Vatican Council in such a way that it would be difficult for Catholic theology to neglect it.[2]

[1] Quoted in "La schéma . . . ," cols. 1401–1402.
[2] See *Constitution on Divine Revelation*, Chapter I, Article 4.

57

The simple repetition, however, of the phrase "Christ is the revelation" does not guarantee that a truly Christological understanding of revelation has been or will be attained. While it has been common in recent years to say that Christ is the revelation, there are few attempts to explain how the use of the word "revelation" in this sense is related to the other uses of the word in Catholic theology. One would suspect that the identification of revelation with Christ is usually not taken in literalness. It is assumed to be a beautiful metaphor indicating that not only the words of Christ taught us about God, but that his activities and attitudes did also. It would be thought, however, that strictly speaking revelation cannot be a person since revelation is truth that God makes known to man.

There is great need to examine what we do mean when we speak of Christ as the revelation. In particular we must, as the *Constitution* indicates, relate this to the revelational-redemptive history of which we have spoken earlier. We cannot be content to say that Christ is simply the last and greatest event of an historical chain. In this chapter I wish rather to assert: 1) that God's revelation not only reaches a high point in Christ but is recapitulated in him; 2) that the participating subject who first receives the Christ-revelation is not the apostolic community but Christ himself; 3) that the fullness of revelation reached at the resurrection cannot perdure in books or institutions but only in the consciousness of the glorified Lord.

GOD TOTALLY REVEALING

We have seen earlier that although God made use of many instruments in the revelational process it was always God who was being revealed. He was present among the people of the Old Testament giving himself to them in a communion of knowledge and love. For a truly personal communion with man,

God had to be God for man in a human way.[3] Since his desire was to manifest a tri-personal life and to reveal to man his share in that life, only a person, only God living a human life, could adequately reveal this. Revelation from the beginning was concerned not so much with problems, facts, or events, but an inner personal life; finally, it was in the flesh of a human nature that the unsuspected and unsurpassable revealing took place.

The Incarnation is not merely a brute fact out of the past. It is the opening of a human history which established a unique way of revelation. This is the true and primary *source of revelation:* God revealing in Christ. Jesus Christ is the gospel that springs up from within the inner life of the triune God.[4] God's speaking to man had always been threatened with becoming an abstract, conceptual word emptied of its meaning. With Jesus Christ, the irreducible, concrete, fleshly word was spoken which expressed all that God wished to say or could say to the world. "The secret of God becomes the secret of man, because this man is God. . . . The light is given, the light is united to men, and this union is not a philosophical system or an inspired book, but is Someone living, the man Jesus Christ."[5] From that moment onward, the expression "word of God" could have only one strict and primary meaning: the personal Word. Every other use of the expression is valid only insofar as it shares in or throws light upon the person of the Word.

That the Old Testament was the revelatory-redemptive preparation for Christ is a Christian belief reaffirmed by the Council.[6] If such a preparation were something more than an external instruction, then we must conceive of Israel as the process and

---

[3] See Karl Rahner, "Die ewige Bedeutung der Menschheit Jesu für unser Gottesverhältnis," *Schriften zur Theologie,* Band III (Einsiedeln, Benziger, 1956), pp. 56–57.

[4] See George Tavard, "Scripture and Tradition: Source or Sources?" in *Journal of Ecumenical Studies,* I (Autumn, 1964), p. 449.

[5] Mersch, *op. cit.,* p. 380.

[6] *Constitution on Divine Revelation,* Chapter I, Article 3.

the partial realization of that body which issued from the Virgin Mary. By successive acts of freeing Israel from her selfish ways, God was preparing mankind for a definitive act of love which would free man from the bondage of flesh. The community itself could not be the bearer of the final revelation, but the community could help to form the one who, flesh of our flesh, could bear for his brothers the final gift of God's personal existence. If this one man were taken up into God's life, it could not help but have an effect upon the entire social body. The diffuse revelational acts of God in the Old Testament were thus contracted into the personal history which stands at the pinnacle of God's dealing with Israel. By Jesus' complete receptivity to the self-bestowing love of God, all that had haltingly and successively been made present in the history of Israel was recapitulated and focused in one life span.[7]

It should hardly be surprising, therefore, that Christ was understood through the images and events of the Old Testament while at the same time he reciprocally threw light upon the ancient books.[8] In reading the Old Testament Christ discovered the elements of his own biography and, conversely, it was in his own person that the separate strands of Old Testament development fused. Christ abolished neither Law, nor Sabbath, nor Temple; he brought them together and brought them to completion by becoming them. In the prophetic tradition and in the wisdom literature Christ (and later the Church) found the imagery and vocabulary to describe his person and his mission. It was not so much in isolated texts of the Old Testament that Christ was to be found, but in the whole flowing movement and development of man's relation to God.

It would also follow from what we have said previously that

[7] See Rudolf Schnackenburg, "Zum Offenbarungsgedanken in der Bibel," in *Biblische Zeitschrift,* VII (January, 1963), p. 6.

[8] See Pierre Grelot, *Sens chrétien de l'Ancien Testament* (Tournai, 1962), pp. 125–165; Aloys Grillmeier, *Christ in Christian Tradition* (New York, Sheed and Ward, 1965), pp. 3–35.

if Christ sums up the history of God's speaking to Israel, he also in some way contains the universal history of God's dealing with man. The Old Testament conceives of the redemptive covenant with Israel as paradigmatic, so that the creation of the universe and universal history are directed toward redemption and contained within the covenant. In viewing cosmic history in this way, 2 Isaiah represents the peak of Old Testament development; it is from that peak that Christ begins. Whatever the ontological consequences that might be drawn from this teaching, the scripture leaves little doubt that the whole of history moved toward its assumption in Christ. All of the words which God had spoken, beginning with the word of creation, are included in the Word who is personally God. What is chronologically first must be understood in the light of the later, full revelation.

Jesus Christ is God, the eternal subsistent Word; his words are the words of God. Nevertheless, God is still revealed in Christ through the veil of human flesh. Even when it is the Son of God in question, truth for man is always a veiling and an unveiling. Through bodily symbols man reveals himself to another, but it is at the same time the body which veils and makes impossible the total unveiling or disposition of the person.[9] When we say, therefore, that Christ is the fullness of revelation we do not mean that God became clearly known to all who looked upon Christ. To most he is a puzzle, to some he is a scandal, to all he is incomprehensible. Even to Christ's most faithful followers God is revealed only partially and temporally and always through human symbols.

God revealed himself in Jesus Christ, but this personal existence incarnated itself in successive gestures and actions, and in human speech which attempts to incarnate thought. His being

[9] See Lucien Jerphagnon, "Le corps et la communication des consciences," in L'homme au regard de la foi (Paris, Les Éditions Ouvrières, 1959), pp. 183–193.

61

shone forth through his words as testimony to what he is. His credibility rested not upon the evidence of his ideas but upon the manifestation of his person. His teaching could not be separated from his person, and although later generations may find it impossible to write a biography of Jesus, his teachings preserved by the Church do give insight into his person.[10]

In addition to his teaching which was revelatory of God, every action, appearance, and gesture of Christ was infinitely rich in meaning.[11] Beyond the logic of his doctrine it was his manner of meeting people, the way he spoke, and his acts of merciful love which revealed the power of God. The miracles which play such a significant part in the scriptural accounts have this function in the revelatory process. They were not given primarily as proofs to convince unbelievers, nor as external testimonies to his teaching. Just as prophecy is the effect of revelation upon history, so miracles are the effect upon man's world of God's revealing presence. "Miracles happen spontaneously because the Kingdom is in the midst of men."[12] Instead of external criteria for judging the word spoken, the miracles are part of the speaking process. Through Christ's miracles there is spoken to the world the power and the love of God and the conflict of good with evil in the world.

There is another point of crucial importance that cannot be neglected when one speaks of God revealing himself in Christ. The revelation of Christ is at one and the same time the revelation of the Trinity. Scripture does not merely say that God appeared, but that "the Father appeared to men in the Son; in fact, that is everything; the whole content of revelation is contained in that, and that is Christ."[13] The role of the Logos-

---

10 See James M. Robinson, *A New Quest for the Historical Jesus* (Naperville, Ill., Allenson, 1959), p. 95.

11 See *Constitution on Divine Revelation*, Chapter I, Article 4.

12 Dumont, *loc. cit.*, p. 136.

13 Mersch, *op. cit.*, p. 376.

revealer seems at first glance to be an ambiguous one. On the one hand, he seems to be the one revealed, the one who is in possession of the truth. On the other hand, he seems more often to point beyond himself as faithful witness to the Father.

To set up an opposition here between a Christocentric and theocentric concept of revelation would be superficial and misleading. The Son is revealed but it is precisely in relation to the Father (and to the Spirit).[14] Whoever sees him sees the Father (Jn. 14:9). The Son is the revelation of the Father and the person within the Trinity who expresses the truth. He is not only "one of the divine persons any of whom could become man if he wanted to, but *the* person in whom God communicates himself hypostatically to the world; the Incarnation mirrors the unique personal character of the second divine person, the Word."[15] Others had spoken about God but the Eternal Logos was the witness who had seen him. No one else knew God in the full biblical sense of knowing. The Son gives this knowledge to whom he wishes (Mt. 11:27) not by explaining the Father, but simply by speaking and acting. Christ in his person reveals the way that men are to take to God; he is the way, the truth, and the life. In revealing himself as the way and the gracious act of God, Christ simultaneously makes known himself, the Father, and the plan of salvation.[16]

CHRIST AS THE RECIPIENT OF REVELATION

That God was in Christ revealing himself to men and that Jesus Christ is God's Word to the world is an affirmation repeatedly made in recent Catholic writing. That the man Jesus was the

[14] See A. Decourtray, "La conception johannique de la foi," in *Nouvelle revue théologique,* LXXXI (June, 1959), p. 567.

[15] Karl Rahner, *Nature and Grace* (New York, Sheed and Ward, 1964), p. 127

[16] See L. Cerfaux, *Christ in the Theology of St. Paul* (New York, Herder and Herder, 1959), pp. 402–418.

recipient of God's revelation and fulfilled the vocation of the man of faith is a statement equally important yet seldom made in Catholic theological writing. It is perhaps one of the unfortunate legacies of the nineteenth and early twentieth centuries (though the problem is much older than that) that orthodox writing tends implicitly to devaluate the humanness of Jesus Christ.

Every Catholic who has had a minimum of religious instruction knows that Christ is truly man and therefore has a human nature. But in our real, existential thinking or in prayer, writes Karl Rahner, we (theologians as well as simple faithful) tend to put the humanity of Christ on God's side not man's.[17] As a result of this, the gospel record of the life of Christ is taken not as the story of a human life but as a piece of play-acting in which nothing really happens and in which the personal reactions are little more than pretension. "Such a piece of play-acting would be unworthy," writes Daniélou, "Christ pretended nothing. He did not pretend to be a man; he really *was* a man."[18] In many theological considerations (for example, of grace, redemption, or sacraments) there has developed a better understanding of the place of Christ's humanity. In the most basic area of revelation, however, there remains (despite appearances and assertions to the contrary) an almost complete void.

This matter of Christ as the recipient or human participant in revelation is of no small importance. It is in fact the key to the personal, social, and historical character of Christian revelation. If our previous analysis is correct, that is, if revelation is found in the intercommunion of God and man, then one must look for the highest expression of this covenant bond and dialogue *in* the Lord Jesus. He is man receiving as well as God bestowing; the very meaning of the Incarnation is this inter-

[17] Rahner, "Die ewige . . . ," pp. 48–49.
[18] Daniélou, *Christ and Us,* p. 123.

course of divine and human. The highest union of God and man is not that between Christ and his apostles; the one perfect union is in the Word which comes from the Father and is united to the humanity of Christ.[19]

Jesus did not present himself as God speaking truths to be written down and learned by men. He did present himself as the one who lived in prayerful communion with the Father and one who invited men to join with him in this communion of knowledge and love. "The whole religious life of Christ was dominated and directed by this personal relation to God, his Father: God revealed and communicated himself interiorly as *his* Father; Christ lived in an ineffable, personal communion, in a permanent 'I-Thou' dialogue with God *his* Father."[20]

As Christ recapitulated the wonderful works of *God*, so too he recapitulated man in all his levels of uniqueness and universality. He is the summation of all that was best in the religious life of mankind. He is the supreme case of the "man who orders his life, his whole existence, upon the real and living word that dominates everything in him, to the point at which he is ultimately 'taken up' into the Word, and bears witness to it with his life and blood."[21] Christ is the first of men whose own existence throws light on all of human existence as it is constituted by a nature that is open upward and perfected in freedom by its nearness to God.[22]

[19] In "The Theology of Revelation" (*Theological Studies,* XXV [March, 1964], p. 47), an article which is mainly a review of Latourelle's book, Avery Dulles criticizes the author's failure to develop this receptiveness of Christ to the revelation of his Father and the elaboration of it in his human consciousness: "Latourelle writes almost as if Christ's human words were a direct expression of His divine consciousness, and gives no attention to the psychological structure of Christ's human intellection."

[20] Juan Alfaro, "Persona y gracia," in *Gregorianum,* XLI (January, 1960), p. 26.

[21] Urs von Balthasar, *Martin Buber and Christianity,* p. 26.

[22] See Karl Rahner, "Current Problems in Christology," in *Theological Investigations,* vol. I, pp. 183–192.

65

One of the most pressing needs of contemporary theology is to work out a theology of Christ's consciousness and psychological development as a complement to the theology expressed in the Chalcedonic categories.[23] Though the topic may seem esoteric and unnecessary for the ordinary Christian, it is a fact nonetheless that if theology fails to provide the concrete data, Christian piety fills in the abstract categories with unexamined and to a large extent erroneous detail. The exegete's task is to trace the development in Christ's life as it is recorded in the historical accounts. The theologian for his part can provide a framework for this study, Catholic theology insisting that a phenomenology of consciousness cannot be entirely separated from a metaphysical structure.

The concrete and detailed study of Christ's knowledge is yet to be written; even the basic principles of that development go beyond what can be covered here. I would insist, however, upon the centrality of this question, upon the truly human character of Christ's knowledge, and upon consciousness as springing up from within human life as a point of receptivity.[24] In the unique consciousness of this unique individual there takes place fully and definitively the encounter of God and man in redemptive revelation. "A new knowledge finds its way into mankind, a knowledge that comes from God himself to man, and springs up in the deepest center of mankind, in the heart of this man who is the heart of the whole race—God gives this knowledge, and it is formed in the God-man, it is human and at the same time divine. It is what we call revelation."[25]

Attempts to speak of the revelation coming to its fullness in the human understanding of Christ are hampered by a superficial

[23] See *ibid.*, pp. 149–168; Bernard Lonergan, "Christ as Subject: A Reply," *Gregorianum*, XL (1959), p. 269.

[24] See Jean Mouroux, *The Mystery of Time* (New York, Desclée, 1964), p. 124.

[25] Mersch, *op. cit.*, p. 395.

understanding of what it means "to know." In a common-sense view of knowing, one either knows a fact or does not know it; the knower possesses a thing called knowledge by looking at a world of objects and seeing it as it is. It does not take much philosophical probing to reveal how inadequate this conception of knowledge is. Modern philosophy has emphasized the difference between knowing an object and knowing a person.[26] Even more fundamental is the difference between the knowledge of another and the knowledge of oneself. Whatever explanations are given for man's self knowledge it is certain that man does not view himself as one among many objects in the universe. Man knows and affirms himself at least implicitly in the affirmation of every individual being. Knowing oneself is not simply the possessing of a fact; it is the taking hold of one's identity in a way which may vary from a simple, global awareness to a detailed, reflexive understanding.

A knower is simply a being capable of reflecting back upon itself and its relation to others. To know is to be aware of and to possess one's self presence. A being with such perfection and power, one that has to some degree emerged from the conditions of the material being dispersed in space and time, we call spiritual. If knowing is simply the perfection of being it does not necessarily imply a split between knower and known; in a being of pure actuality, knowing and being would be identical. For man, the finite and material being, knowing is always mediated by what is other than himself. Although there is a basic presence to self which inclines man toward knowing, he is born without any actual knowledge. The conjunction of the capacity or thirst for knowledge with bodily presence to the world brings him into conscious reflexive presence to himself and others.[27]

[26] See Chapter 8.
[27] See Maréchal, *op. cit.*, pp. 105–125; Carlos Cirne-Lima, *Personal Faith* (New York, Herder and Herder, 1965), pp. 61–135.

Concerning Christ's knowledge, theologians have long wrestled with several problems, particularly: 1) the question of the beatific vision; 2) the possibility of ignorance, development, and experiential knowledge—all three of which are closely related and all three apparently excluded by the beatific vision; 3) the presence of infused knowledge.

Catholic teaching has strongly defended the thesis that Christ always had a consciousness of his divine sonship. The question which has divided theologians has been the manner in which Christ had this "vision." Too often, however, it has been assumed that Christ possessed the facts of who he was and there was nothing more to learn, that he had a vision of God which excluded any real growth in knowledge. The word "vision" here is partly responsible for this misunderstanding since it seems to assume an object presented from the outside and looked at. Christ would not have gained a knowledge of God by objective data being presented to him. Such a conception springs from the reduction of knowledge to a looking out upon the world of objective fact. Christ's human nature was immediately present to the Word through the hypostatic union. Since this union is an act of a spiritual being at its highest point, the reality of this union cannot be entirely unconscious. Christ was present to God because he was present to himself. The basic self-identity and self-presence that is the *a priori* of objective and conceptual knowledge implies that Christ knew himself in every act of objective knowing. Thus God was attained in the human understanding of Christ as the first reality known and as always known insofar as a knower knows himself at least implicitly in his knowledge of any other thing.[28]

If this is the way in which Christ's consciousness attained to

[28] See Rahner, "Current Problems . . . ," *loc. cit.,* pp. 169–170; for a general summary of these points as discussed in contemporary theology, see A. Grillmeier, "The Figure of Christ in Catholic Theology Today," in *Theology Today,* vol. I: *Renewal in Dogma* (Milwaukee, Bruce, 1965), pp. 66–108.

the knowledge of God, it is possible for him to have been ignorant of objective facts. He stood in need of the knowledge which comes through temporal and bodily existence in the world with other men. The peculiar mark of human knowledge is that despite a drive toward the plenitude of being, man's specific, actual knowledge is gained only through and in bodily experience. Christ's presence to the Logos did not provide any objective, communicable knowledge. He had to experience the world to acquire his explicit knowledge of factual situations.[29]

There should, therefore, be no great problem in attributing ignorance and thereby real human development in Christ. The history of his self-expression was not only the history of his psychological adaptation to his surroundings, but a human growth in understanding and knowledge. There were certainly limits to Christ's knowledge; the question is the way in which the limitation is to be conceived. It would not help to imagine a large body of numerable facts, some of which Christ had and some of which he did not have. Rather, within the perspective indicated above, Christ's knowledge is a presence to himself which is at once a consciousness of God and a global awareness of all that is related to God. Such a relation in knowledge not only does not exclude a development of knowledge, but demands as its necessary complement the emergence of conceptual and communicable knowledge.[30]

Contemporary theology's insistence upon the limitations of Christ's knowledge is not intended to denigrate his greatness as man. Christ possessed human knowledge to an extraordinary degree, but it was *human* knowledge, that is partial, temporal, and experiential. Whereas medieval theology thought that it

[29] See A. Durand, "La science du Christ," in *Nouvelle revue théologique,* LXXI (May, 1949), p. 500.

[30] See Jean Galot, "Science et conscience de Jésus," in *Nouvelle revue théologique,* LXXXII (February, 1960), pp. 112–115; F. X. Durrwell, *The Resurrection* (New York, Sheed and Ward, 1960), p. 134, n. 51; Karl Adam, *Christ of Faith* (New York, Mentor Omega Books, 1957), p. 312.

was fitting to attribute all gifts and all knowledge to Christ's humanity, we realize today that it is more fitting and more accurate to see Christ living his human life as the recapitulation of man's revelational history, like to us in all things save sin. Whereas medieval theology made no distinction between an immediate knowledge of God and the "beatific vision," contemporary theology attributes to Christ a direct knowledge of God that is not necessarily beatifying while he is on earth.[31]

The so-called "infused knowledge" traditionally asserted of Christ's consciousness cannot be deduced from his divine sonship. Some theologians assert that this knowledge is required by Christ's redemptive mission. The gospels show Christ with an extraordinary prophetic or messianic knowledge that perhaps requires some special illumination in addition to his knowledge by experience. This knowledge would not have to be conceived of as a pouring of concepts into his consciousness, but rather as the providing of an impetus to a special insight into the knowledge implicit in him by reason of who he was. The extent and nature of any infused knowledge remains an open question exegetically and theologically, but the question is at any rate not central to the main concern of this chapter.[32]

The revelation of God to mankind was thus formed in the conscious human experience of Jesus Christ, sustained by his love. His awareness of God was embedded in the patterns appropriate to each stage of his life so that there was continuous growth. He advanced in wisdom and age and favor before both God and man. Having gone out from the Father in the likeness

---

[31] See Engelbert Gutwenger, *Bewusstsein und Wissen Christi* (Innsbruck, Felizian Rauch, 1960), pp. 150–155; Durand, *loc. cit.,* pp. 498–503; on the Church's teaching relative to the ignorance of Christ, see Galot, *loc. cit.,* p. 127.

[32] See Galot, *loc. cit.,* pp. 125–126; Gutwenger, *op. cit.,* pp. 133–144; Karl Rahner, "Dogmatic Considerations on Knowledge and Consciousness in Christ," in *Dogmatic vs. Biblical Theology,* edited by Herbert Vorgrimler (Baltimore, Helicon, 1964), p. 263.

of sinful flesh, he experienced the pain and suffering of his return journey. Son though he was, he learned obedience by the things he suffered. Suffering worked upon, drawing out the deepest resources of his heroism. Day by day he was able to gather more clearly the details of his coming passion. He did not attempt to escape from the human situation, but wished to experience and ratify it in its completeness. He came in fulfillment of the lineage of great Old Testament prophets with an attitude similar to theirs but rising above them. "What the Jews should always have done," writes Guardini, "but actually did so seldom, i.e., ascend by faith above immediate, tangible nature to the realm of the mind and the spirit so as to become what God desired them to be, had finally become accomplished in Christ."[33]

To say that Christ lived by vision but that his followers live by faith is true, but it can also be misleading. If we conceive of faith as the patient acceptance of what God wills over what man desires, Jesus' fundamental human attitude was the same as that of the true servant of Yahweh and the faithful Christian. The Christian's life of faith means an imitation and a following of him on the road of obedience. Though Catholic theology denies that Christ had the theological virtue of faith, he is nevertheless the archetype and ideal of faith. His knowledge was measured by his mission; his "hour" was untouchable both by his enemies and by himself. He lived in the sheer, naked, unqualified acceptance of what came from the Father.[34]

FULLNESS OF REVELATION: THE GLORIFIED CHRIST

The story of the gospel moves inexorably toward its climax. The double theme of Son revealing the Father and Father

[33] Romano Guardini, *The Humanity of Christ* (New York, Pantheon, 1964), p. 79.
[34] See Urs von Balthasar, *Theology of History*, pp. 30–32.

71

glorifying the Son finds its perfect fusion at "the hour" to which his life pointed. It was at that hour that God's love for man encountered the total responsiveness of man's love; at that hour the revelation-redemption was accomplished.

Throughout his life Christ had taught, healed, comforted, preached, but all of these symbols were inadequate to express what he was. Like other men, Christ knew more than he could say; he was more than he could consciously grasp. His self-expression through word and action awaited the most perfect expression of the cross. "All that was incommunicable in the divine communication expresses itself in the arms outstretched, the body emptied of blood and the heart pierced by the centurion's lance (Jn. 19:34). The word of love was given over fully to man. The revelation by word was consummated and sealed by revelation in action."[35]

The final action of his life was the event which recapitulated his history just as his life recapitulated the whole revelational history. In that one act there was concentrated the supreme revelation of God's self-gift to the world. God gave him up to death to reveal the face of his glory. Death, which had been the sign of sin in the world (Rom. 5:12), became the expression of divine love and the revelation of divine grace.[36]

In addition to being the final revelation of God's love, the cross is the final revelation of the power of evil in man, of man's emptiness, and of man's need for redemption. With Christ's death sin was revealed in all of its horror. Sinful man is frightened of love, he is frightened of freedom, and most of all he is frightened of God. The one time in our history, therefore, that the divine appeared in all of his love and freedom, could have only one result. Sinful flesh could not endure it

[35] Latourelle, *op. cit.,* p. 341.
[36] See Karl Rahner, *On the Theology of Death* (New York, Herder and Herder, 1961), p. 78.

and so the Christ had to suffer and die (Lk. 24:26). To be Son of God in a sinful race was a terrifying thing.

If the cross represented the supreme revelatory action on God's part, it must also have been the supreme act of participating receptivity on the part of man. There is no revelation unless there is a human consciousness taking part in it receptively and answering to God. Clearly, it was not the apostles who were here the recipients; it was the one who as main participant in the action on Calvary offered his life for his brothers. With cries of agony in the Garden and on the cross (Lk. 22:42–44; Mk. 15:34), Christ passed through a kind of dark night of the soul to the final reception of revelation. Having entered the struggle in behalf of the true destiny of mankind, having perceived what was necessary to set man free, he was obedient to the will of his Father, obedient to the death of the cross. He ascended the cross as man's answer to God, but not without suffering, fear, and the desire to let the chalice pass. "We are astounded, we are shocked at this weakness and longing; it would have been more heroic, we feel, to accept unmoved this death which was to save the world. But this astonishment is born of a lack of understanding. We forget that the drama of mankind in search of salvation was first played out in Christ, and that he himself was the first to be raised by the Father."[37]

Revelation reached its fullness, therefore, only at *the* hour when Christ burst through the gates of death by handing over the Spirit (Jn. 19:30). At that moment the redemption of the world was accomplished in his flesh, and revelation as the cognitive expression of redemption was brought to perfection in the consciousness of Christ: he beheld the glory that was his. Though in a sense Christ had already possessed all, there was yet genuine novelty in his exaltation in glory: "When the hour comes and the Father gives it to him as supreme gift of his love, the Son will not say to the Father that he has always

[37] Durrwell, *Resurrection*, p. 57.

known this hour, that it holds nothing new for him, brings only what has been familiar, what he has already savored through and through in thought, already handled and thumbed over in his mind."[38]

In this high point of revelation, therefore, death was but one aspect of the total act. What was from our side death was from the Father's side resurrection. Opening himself completely to God, Christ was transformed by the inrushing Spirit. The reception of Christ into glory is the never to be surpassed event in the revelational process. The resurrection was not only an event of the past; it was the beginning of a new life and the beginning of the total revelation in the risen Christ. Fixed in the act of redeeming us, he continues to offer his life for his brethren, and he continues to receive the revealing and redeeming love of the Father for all mankind.

When viewed in this perspective the time of the "forty days" takes on a much greater significance. "The mode of time revealed during the forty days remains the foundation for every other mode of his presence in time, in the Church, and in the world."[39] A new mode of existence and a new mode of time were contracted into the first born from the dead and shone forth during the paschal time. Christ was now able to bring to light the meaning of words and deeds that his disciples could not previously understand. He had instructed them before his resurrection, but now he had to make them recall these things in the light of the Spirit. The resurrection was for the apostles not so much a proof of his divinity as the light of understanding which was cast upon all the facts of his life. The forty days was a time for instruction but not all was spoken in word, for there is a communication deeper than words can convey. There is noticeable in the post-resurrectional scenes a striking emphasis on eating and drinking, seeing and touching.

[38] Urs von Balthasar, *Theology of History*, p. 31.
[39] *Ibid.*, p. 84.

74

In the psyche of the risen Lord revelation was received (or taken part in receptively) in fullness not only for himself but for all his brothers. At the end of the forty days and then the pentecostal experience, the apostles had received the revelational communion of God's love. They did not receive it, however, in the same way and to the same extent as Christ did (and does). If God's revelation is not to fall off from its high point, it must remain in the one consciousness where it is totally accomplished. The risen and glorified Lord is the one place where revelation continues to happen in fullness.

The Church of time is a Church *en route* toward reunion with Christ in the vision of the blessed. But even while in time the Church is not cut off from that consciousness. Christ remains present to his Church as mediator of her revelation and redemption. "He 'goes before' first as a pillar of fire and then as a presence which moved from Jerusalem to Samaria to the ends of the earth. He is always ahead of the Church, beckoning it to get up to date, never behind it waiting to be refurbished."[40]

Many books say that Christ revealed God during his historical life; some books say that he will reveal God in heaven; but few books say that he is *now revealing* God. This is most unfortunate. At the resurrection Christ was constituted Son of God for us; at that time he *began* his revelatory-redemptive activity in fullness. The Church must take seriously her continuing life in world history so as to understand what God is asking of her at each moment. There is no question of adding objective truths to the deposit of faith, nor is there question of going beyond Christ. What is of utmost importance is that the revelational process first accomplished in Christ should now be participated in by all Christians through a continuing revelational process.

It is a remarkable fact that whereas Catholic writing on grace

[40] Harvey Cox, *The Secular City* (New York, Macmillan, 1965), pp. 147–148.

75

and redemption leaves no doubt that the process of sanctification goes on in our world (without detriment to the once for
all and final character of the redemption on Calvary), there is
a great hesitancy to affirm a continuing revelational process in
our world. This second, however, is just as necessary and just
as important as the first. Unless both are affirmed and both
joined in the risen Lord, there is bound to be a splintering of
Catholic faith and theology into separate compartments of
truths. What Jungmann has shown to be the disastrous effects
of separating grace from the risen Christ is at least as true of
the separation of revelation from the same risen Lord.[41] A faith
that is personal, social, and historical cannot spring from the
acts of God in the Old Testament, nor the accounts of the
historical Christ; rather, "this faith is the result of the *actual,*
present, self-revelation of the heavenly Christ *through* his Spirit
in the Church."[42]

With the passage of this person through history and the
contraction of time within his glorified person, the norm of
history was revealed to be not an abstract law but a person. He
is the norm of our concrete history, both that of the individual
and that of the race; he is the one "concrete-universal." The
truth, the law, the good were revealed not as external criteria
for judging the person, but as realized in the person. This
is the way in which Christ is the final standard of human
entelechy. Man's whole bodily self is to be lifted up to God
in the light and power of that one bodily existence lifted above
and drawing all things.[43]

[41] Jungmann, *The Good News* . . . , pp. 38–55.
[42] Edward Schillebeeckx, "Exegesis, Dogmatics and the Development of
Dogma," in *Dogmatic vs. Biblical Theology,* p. 128.
[43] See *Constitution on Divine Revelation,* Chapter V, Article 17.

IV.

The Apostolic Sharing
in Christ's Consciousness

THE apostles whom Christ chose to follow him during his lifetime and who were witnesses to his resurrection obviously occupy a unique and central place in the process of Christian revelation.[1] Catholic and Protestant theologians agree on the importance of the apostolic experience, yet differ rather widely on the precise significance of it. In this chapter I would like to treat of: 1) the privileged position of the apostles; 2) the nature of their own revelatory experience; 3) the objectification of revelation in their teaching.

THE PRIVILEGED POSITION OF THE APOSTLES

The apostles occupied a unique and unrepeatable role in the constitution and history of the Church. They experienced in their lifetime the man who is personally God. To see him was to see the Father (Jn. 14:9), though not all who looked upon him really did see him (Jn. 6:40). The apostolic experience of Christ is the root which forever grounds the Church's life. When I insisted in the last chapter upon the consciousness of Christ as the place of fullness of revelation, my intention was

[1] See *Constitution on Divine Revelation,* Chapter II, Article 7.

not to lessen the importance of the apostles, but simply to situate their role better.

Jesus presented himself as faithful witness to the Father; at the same time he prepared a band of followers to be his witnesses. Throughout his public ministry he could not say to them all that he wished, for they were yet incapable of understanding it. But his teaching and his person were presented in such a way that the apostles when later reflecting upon him and gaining new insight did not think of themselves as passing to something entirely new. They thus moved easily from belief in Jesus as Messiah to belief in his divinity without seeming to add to their earliest belief in him.

Demanding acceptance of himself as the promised one of Israel, Jesus was asking for a surrender to his person that was already a going beyond the human and could only be realized by the working of grace.[2] The apostles did not simply receive a teaching; they experienced and believed in a person whose words, gestures, actions, and attitudes were symbolic manifestations of the divine. This privileged position, nevertheless, did not exempt them from the burden of following him in darkness, from seeing and listening yet usually not understanding. Despite the fact that God's love was visible in the world, there was in this love a call to go beyond the visible and to see with another kind of vision.[3]

Some faint light had been given to the apostles during Christ's lifetime as indeed a light was already present in the Old Testament. But it was only when the Word was lifted up into another sphere that this faint light erupted into brilliance. In and through his death Christ established with his Church the knowledge of mutual and total self-giving. After the resurrection-ascension-Pentecost the mystery could now be understood

[2] See Jean Levie, "Le message de Jésus dans la pensée des apôtres," in *Nouvelle revue théologique*, LXXXIII (January, 1961), pp. 32–34.

[3] See Rahner, "Die ewige . . . ," *loc. cit.*, p. 48.

by the apostles, the prophets, and all the sanctified. By believing in Christ the apostles dwelt in the light; they received the light into themselves and at the same time were received into it.

Holy Scripture represents this belief as the work of the Spirit of Christ, "the Spirit who brings the wisdom of God into the mind of man, and without ceasing to be the Spirit of God, he is present in the minds of the faithful. In this way he can communicate to them the mysteries of which he has such a deep knowledge."[4] The interior testimony of the Holy Spirit is not an extra guarantee, nor a necessary correlate to revelation. It is, on the contrary, the very heart of the revelational process. The Spirit which had been given to the Messiah, yet not such as to reveal him in glory during his earthly life, was let loose at Pentecost. The Spirit then revealed the Son to the apostles by bringing to light the meaning of the events and words of his life.

The apostles could now delve into the secrets of God's designs because they possessed the understanding of Christ. This phrase "understanding of Christ" is somewhat ambiguous. It might be taken only in the objective sense of having knowledge concerning Christ. St. Paul and St. John meant something more than this. Primarily, it is the very sharing in the subjective consciousness of Christ that is in question; he is the Wisdom that was communicated to the apostolic understanding. The apostles not only looked at him, they looked with him and in him toward the Father. In the consciousness of Christ the Word was spoken in all its clarity. To the apostles it was communicated partially and temporally through their participation "in Christ." The apostles did not proclaim their message as an end in itself; they called not for belief in the truths of their message but for belief in God raising up Christ. The precise formulation of the kerygma was not what was primary because "Paul's thought joins that of Peter and John and together they are subordinated

[4] Cerfaux, op. cit., p. 270.

79

to the thought of Christ."[5] The force and validity of their message came from the fact that it was not theirs but was received through their incorporation into the Body of Christ.

All of this may seem to be obvious; yet there is an irrepressible tendency to move revelation outward from its deepest origin to more objectified expressions. Thus we move from the Father, to Christ, to the apostles, to the apostolic preaching, to the Bible, to Church teachings, to Christian doctrine books. Each of these has a role in the revelational process, but in attempting to reground the meaning of revelation we must trace through the whole process from its source. Catholic writing is more firmly rooted in the Bible today and even in the kerygma within the Bible; but unless it is recognized that these are still partial expressions of a deeper reality, there will be a tendency to fall back into an "oracular revelation" of impersonal truths. The base of revelation and the point to which our considerations must constantly return is the relation between Father and Son, the sending of the Holy Spirit, and the apostolic sharing in the life and knowledge proper to the Son.

The apostles' task was a precarious one; as simple human beings they were to represent the God-man among their fellows. This they were to do not because of their talents, but because of an obedience entrusted to them. "On the one hand, they stand in a position of authority and freedom toward the world and the community. On the other hand, however, as members of the Church they stand in the Church and *under* Christ; they must appear before Christ's judgment and they are dependent on his grace."[6]

The apostles were "servants of the Word," but Word now taken to mean primarily the personal Word who is Son. It was

[5] Jean Levie, *The Bible, Word of God in Words of Men* (New York, P. J. Kenedy and Sons, 1961), p. 300.
[6] Küng, *Structures* . . . , p. 177.

to the resurrected Lord and not only to the fact of resurrection that the apostles gave witness. In trying to pronounce the Word of God they were attempting a task which goes beyond all human capabilities. If the Word were a verbal utterance, men could control such a Word and pass it on simply by speaking. But if the Word is a person, there are no words which can express that one Word. Only with a personal life could one give something of an adequate testimony. The apostolic mission, therefore, as consequent upon the mission of the Son, was not primarily a conveying of words but a presence of person. Through the apostles' lives of faith in the world, men were brought face to face with the Lord in the power of his resurrection.[7]

The Nature of the Apostolic Experience

It will perhaps be instructive to inquire further into the nature of the apostolic experience to understand what revelation meant in their lives. I have previously insisted that all revelation is a communion of intersubjectivity. After the unique case of the divine-human relationship in Jesus Christ, the apostles offer the most striking example for this notion of revelation. Before inquiring into the experience of the ordinary Christian we can profit from examining more carefully the experience of the apostles who according to Catholic teaching were given the whole of revelation for the benefit of the future Church.

The apostolic experience of revelation may be treated in relation to modern discussion on whether revelation is knowledge or whether it is something more or other than knowledge. In contemporary Protestant writing there is frequent assertion that revelation does not consist in facts, truths, or knowledge. With some qualifications similar statements are common among Catholic writers. These latter, of course, defend the part that

[7] See Durrwell, *Resurrection,* p. 309.

81

knowledge plays, but they assert that revelation is not only knowledge; it is *also* encounter, saving actions, personal relation, etc.[8] This juxtaposition raises more questions than it answers, however. It is not very helpful and it could be very harmful to depreciate knowledge in favor of something else if the something else is poorly understood.

At first glance the modern rebellion against conceiving of revelation as knowledge seems rather strange if one considers the biblical testimony. "To St. John," Durrwell remarks in this connection, "salvation was of the order of knowledge as well as of life, and the first effect of the Easter mystery was an illumination. Christ had long ago declared that his paschal exaltation would be the beginning of a new knowledge."[9] St. John was not alone here. St. Paul is no less insistent that the Christian life advances by steps of knowledge and that the inward remaking of a man is an advance in knowledge. (See Eph. 3:17–19; Col. 2:2–3; Phil. 3:7–8.) Both the Fathers of the Church and the great scholastic theologians remained faithful to this tradition. Revelation was conceived of as an illumination, an imprint of the divine intellect upon man's knowing power.[10] Indeed, on scholastic principles it does not seem possible to go beyond truth and knowledge, for knowledge is the highest possession of a spiritual being, or more precisely, it is the very being of a spirit either to share in the truth or to be the Truth.

On the other hand, however, it is not difficult to grasp what contemporary writers on revelation are dissatisfied with. They are opposed to a revelation defined in terms of a certain number of truths to be believed. There is a strong distrust in our day of any system of propositions about God. To speak of

[8] See Latourelle, *op. cit.*, p. 474.

[9] Durrwell, *Resurrection*, p. 204.

[10] See *Summa Theologica*, IIa-IIae, q. 1, a. 1; *Summa Contra Gentiles*, III, c. 40.

revelation as knowledge seems to reduce it to a human possession apart from God. What contemporary writers look to is a
revelation which involves man, the historical and social being,
and not the mind or abstract reason.

We might sympathize with this desire to think of revelation
as not merely a collection of facts, ideas, and concepts, but we
may still question the wisdom of depreciating "mere knowledge"
or "intellectual assent." It is easy to be against abstractions and
rationalisms, but opposition to them does not overcome them.
Indeed, as modern philosophers have pointed out, every attempt
to overcome rationalism at its own level, every attempt to destroy
rationalism simply by opposing it, ends by creating a new and
often worse rationalism.[11] The way to overcome superficial understanding and worthless knowledge is not by opposing them
but by achieving a deeper understanding and more meaningful
knowledge.

The program which many modern philosophers have set for
themselves, namely, to reground knowledge in a radical, stricter
kind of thinking, must also be the concern of a Catholic theology
of revelation. I do not think that the word "knowledge" in
reference to divine revelation should be given up or even reduced to a secondary role. I admit that those who speak of
revelation being more than mere knowledge are using the word
"knowledge" differently from the way I use it here. This is not,
however, a quibbling over the definition of words. Whereas
they tend to equate knowledge with words and concepts, or
rather with static entities cut off from the real world, I deny that
this equation should be made; further, I deny that it is by
chance that it has been made. This use of words is a direct
consequence of our failure to investigate truth and knowledge
at the level at which they must be understood. The question of
truth and knowledge is of incalculable importance both theo-

[11] See Martin Heidegger, *An Introduction to Metaphysics* (New York,
Doubleday Anchor Books, 1961), p. 103.

logically and pastorally. It cannot be dismissed in favor of something else supposedly more real, concrete, and personal. "The fact that I will be known, acknowledged and loved is *my* fulfillment. And this fulfillment in knowledge and love—in being known and being loved—is not merely a fulfillment on the 'intentional plane' but rather the fulfillment of the reality, of the being itself."[12]

For a theology of revelation the question will in large part be the recovery of the biblical meaning of "knowing God." It has often been remarked in scriptural writing that the biblical word "know" has a much richer meaning than our word. It is not always brought out, however, that this is no biblical peculiarity or curious bit of information. On the meaning of "know" the Bible was right—in a somewhat naïve and unphilosophical way, while most of our philosophical and theological presentations have been wrong or at least woefully inadequate. When this has been admitted, however, there can be no question of attacking "Greek categories" and returning to a Semitic outlook. The recovery of the biblical meaning of "know" cannot proceed by way of a return to a simple, unreflexive attitude, but must take place through a deeper reflection that will lead to a new integration.

We have indicated that knowledge must not be superficially conceived as a "taking a look at the already-out-there-now." What is obvious in knowing is looking, but we are wrong in assuming, writes Lonergan, "that what is obvious in knowing is what knowing obviously is."[13] Knowledge tends to be identified with the concepts and words without which there is no human knowledge. But if human knowledge is the inner presence of being to itself mediated by its relation to the other, then neither the concept nor the word is knowledge itself but

[12] Karl Rahner, "Priest and Poet," in *The Word. Readings in Theology,* compiled at the Canisianum (New York, P. J. Kenedy and Sons, 1964), p. 9.
[13] Lonergan, *op. cit.,* p. 416.

both are intrinsic elements in a knowing process. The dynamism of man's intellect leads to a "lived knowledge," a unity of knower and known. This union is brought to full reflexive consciousness only by progressive conceptual expression and dialogue.[14]

What may seem to be only philosophical technicality is of the utmost importance here. A "common-sense scholasticism" in which truth and knowledge were assumed to be found in the linking together of concepts has had disastrous effects when applied to the theology of revelation, the development of doctrine, inerrancy of Scripture, and numerous other questions in theology. What is needed is a deeper originating point than that where knowledge is the function of a faculty and truth is a function of statements. "Knowledge is life: *cognoscere cognoscentibus est esse*. Supernatural knowledge is life at its fullest; it is eternal life: 'This is eternal life, that they may know.' (Jn. 17:3)."[15]

If we return now to our central concern of the apostles and revelation we may be able to make more intelligible the statement that the apostles witnessed to the whole of revelation for the future Church. Such a grasp of the revelation was obviously not in the form of conceptual expression and explicit judgment, but it was nonetheless a knowing experience. As we have seen, "the object of the act of understanding is the intelligible; the intelligible is expressed in concepts, but its basic occurrence is prior to the concept."[16] As natural knowledge proceeds from participation in the divine light whereby the first principles of knowledge are present to the intellect, so too it was the indwelling Spirit who made potentially and implicitly present to the apostles the whole of revelation. This special gift of the Spirit coupled with

[14] See Maréchal, *op. cit.*, pp. 22–29; William A. Luijpen, *Existential Phenomenology* (Pittsburgh, Duquesne University, 1963), pp. 103–104.
[15] Mersch, *op. cit.*, p. 86.
[16] Lonergan, "Christ . . . ," *loc. cit.*, p. 262.

the apostles' immediate experience of Christ, especially after the Resurrection, brought to an extraordinary degree of fruition the life of knowledge in the Holy Spirit.

The apostolic possession of (or being possessed by) the whole of Christian revelation did not rest upon their penetrating through a maze of concepts and doctrines. There was a living bond between their understanding and the existential orbit of their lives. There was a lived judgment which established them in the truth before conceptual judgments were formed. The formulation of explicit judgments always presupposes the more fundamental pre-predicative comprehension of truth. For the apostles this meant that there was a pre-predicative experience of presence in the Spirit which was gradually formulated into conceptual knowledge directed by and at the same time illuminating their experience of the Word.

Attaining the truth of revelation for the apostles depended first of all not upon the correct joining of concepts, but upon their fundamental option for Truth, that is, the God of Truth. For this reason, St. John and many Church Fathers understand the opposite of truth to be not error but "the Father of lies." For the apostolic believers, to stand in the truth did not rest so much upon their degree of intelligence as upon the openness at the center of their being to God's Spirit. For the unbelievers, on the other hand, it was not the presentation of doctrine that was lacking, but their receptiveness to the Father's gift.[17]

THE OBJECTIFICATION OF APOSTOLIC REVELATION

In insisting upon the pre-predicative, pre-conceptual basis of the revelation to the apostles, I have no intention of denying the necessity and importance of the conceptual, the judgmental, and the verbal. Man cannot bring to reflexive awareness his lived

---

[17] See Decourtray, *loc. cit.,* p. 562; Schnackenburg, "Zum Offenbarungs-gedanken . . . ," *loc. cit.,* p. 16.

truth without the mediation of objective expressions. The modernist error was to suppose that religious experience is an inner reality of the individual and that the objective expression is a more or less detachable part not intrinsic to the experience itself. But bodily expression in the objective world is not something outside of man, unimportant to intellectual knowledge or religious experience. Man does not have a body as a kind of instrument; man is bodily by nature with a bodiliness that is distinct from spirit and yet the fulfillment of it.[18] The apostolic revelational experience was thus always bodied forth in concepts, words, and other objective expressions.

The preaching of God's message would have been impossible if it were not for concepts and judgments. Each concept is an advance and a dynamic tendency in which perceived data are set against the total horizon. Each concept points beyond itself so that at each stage of development more is contained in the expression than the conceptual content reveals. Conceptualization is an attempt to express various aspects of a known reality; such an attempt is always "an infinite search which approaches its goal only asymptotically."[19]

The apostles knew more than they could say; they knew more than they could reflexively bring before their own minds. A man who experiences something deeply finds his words insufficient to express what he means. He gropes for phrases and images, all of which do not "contain" his experience. Yet because they are never adequate to his knowledge it would be erroneous to suppose that they are therefore false. Worse still would it be to try to avoid or suppress this objectifying process. Although words and concepts must live from something deeper than themselves and although they constantly threaten to be-

---

[18] Rahner, *Geist in Welt,* p. 80; Bernard Lonergan, "Cognitional Structure," in *Continuum,* II (Autumn, 1964), pp. 540–542.

[19] Rahner, "Development of Dogma," in *Theological Investigations,* vol. I, p. 64.

come a veiling rather than a revealing instrument, experience cannot avoid objectification as part of the process of becoming fully human. The objective expression is not only necessary in order to reveal something to another; it is the means by which experience becomes clarified for the subject himself.

"Mere conceptualization" is not to be attacked, therefore, since this is to attack the human condition. Concepts are rather to be understood within an originating, primitive, cognitive intention which carries the knowing process forward. A continuous process of differentiation and integration gradually fills out man's "pre-grasp" or drive toward the plenitude of being. Such a development never takes place simply within a subject faced by objects but always involves a dialectical interplay between subjects in a community.

One of the strongest forces drawing out man's knowledge into a full human reality is the symbol of language which embodies a whole history of intersubjective experience. Language, on the obvious level, is a tool forged by man, a supple instrument to be manipulated by him. More deeply considered, language appears as a "given" of man's nature. Similar to other symbolic expressions but probably more than any other of them, language stands in reciprocal relationship to man's life and helps to forge the individual consciousness and its religious experience. "Living man is a man on the way, a way that consists of continually re-establishing a balance that keeps destroying itself. Speech is a particularly valuable symbol of this perpetual movement of a human being, a movement that is opposed to any definitive formulation."[20] The language which the apostles spoke was not then a kind of container into which revelation was poured or placed. Their language, with all of its peculiar characteristics, was one of the direct, continuing casual influences in the apostolic revelational experience.

[20] Georges Gusdorf, *Speaking* (Evanston, Northwestern University, 1965), p. 87.

Viewing knowledge in this total perspective, we have no cause to be surprised by the continued revelation in the primitive Church (D 783), a growth in revelation that was qualitatively different from that in the post-apostolic Church. This growth was neither the occasional intrusion of the Spirit to add some new fact or truth, nor was it only the logical explication of truths already received. Given the bestowal of the Spirit and the character of human knowledge, the apostolic growth in revelation had to continue as long as the apostles lived simply because human reflection and objectification is a lifelong process.

There existed in the primitive Church a delicate balance between, on the one hand, the prophetic light and the prepredicative experience of the individual person, and, on the other hand, the institutional framework and objective formulations. No human project could perdure without some objective structure, but until the end of the apostolic period the detailed working out of that structure remained in question. The primitive Church, through the direction of the apostles and also the "prophets" (Eph. 2:20), formed itself into the permanent ground and norm for all future ages. The Spirit who worked in the primitive community exercised a qualitatively unique influence upon these unique and privileged witnesses. The Spirit did not speak on his own authority but called to mind and interpreted what the Lord had said. Thus, while the apostles were already showing forth in their persons and words the revelatory action of God, the Spirit was at the same time bringing to better reflexive awareness from within the community the meaning of their experience.[21]

When the early Church realized that the final appearance of the Lord might not be imminent, the need for a full objective structure became more obvious. The primitive Church as norm

[21] See *Constitution on Divine Revelation*, Chapter V, Article 19; and also Karl Rahner, *Inspiration in the Bible* (New York, Herder and Herder, 1961), pp. 45–46.

for future ages was to pass down a structure within which the revelational process could continue. Not only books and buildings were to be handed on; it was a communally and hierarchically structured Church in which the Spirit dwelt that the apostolic community bequeathed to their successors. What had taken place in the consciousness of Christ and had been shared in by the apostolic community was never to be surpassed, but neither was it to cease since Christ had come for all men. The Spirit once given was never to be retracted; he continues to cry with longing within the heart of the Church: "Come Lord Jesus" (Apoc. 22:20). As the first community shared in this consciousness in the Spirit, so all Christians are to participate in the experience of the apostles, that is, the experience of Christ in the Spirit.

It was precisely to insure that the Spirit of Jesus would be recognized and that the revelational experience could be continued that a "deposit" was constituted, an objective structure which guarantees the revelational process. I will speak in the following chapter of the written deposit. Here I will merely make mention of the transferral of office within the community.

The apostolic office is, of course, unique. Only one group of men was witness to the life, death, and resurrection of Jesus. It was they alone who were chosen by Christ to be the foundational pillars of his Church. The apostles, however, were also the first pastors in the Church and this office they handed over to their post-apostolic successors. The ministers who continue to serve are to be servants of the Word—witnesses not primarily to the preached or written word, but to the glorified Lord still present in his Church through his Spirit.[22]

The continuity in the Church stems from the continuing consciousness in the Spirit preserved and guided by the objective structure that is its necessary complement. A hierarchically structured community remains the objective expression for a

[22] See *Constitution on Divine Revelation*, Chapter V, Article 17.

revelation always being given by God and always being received by man. Revelation is not something given to bishops, priests, and other teachers to be dispensed by them. Never is revelation something possessed and handed down, stated in books or solidified in creeds. We never take possession of him, rather, he comes to repossess us for God.[23]

This leads our consideration to a distinction made in most Catholic writing on this topic, one between "mediate revelation" and "immediate revelation." It is usually said that prophets and apostles received God's revelation immediately but that all others receive revelation only through human intermediaries.[24] Undoubtedly, it is true that the apostles have an immediacy here which is denied to those of a later era; this immediacy needs definition, however, so as not to distort the differences. From our previous analysis of the historical, personal, and social character of revelation we may suggest some remarks relative to this distinction between mediate and immediate revelation.

First of all, it is not at all evident that the apostolic (as also the prophetic) experience is without a mediacy that includes other men. Revelation, insofar as it is historical and personal, is always to some degree a communal experience. It would be naïve to suppose that the prophet or apostle received "divine truths" by an unmediated gift of God and that revelation was independent of their own cultural or personal relationships. The supposition that something (that is, revelation) was given to them unmediated by personal experience, reflection, interpretation, and communal life cannot be sustained. This mediating element applies also to the very words of Christ. These words communicated a conscious experience in the apostles' lives that

---

[23] See Küng, *Structures of the Church*, p. 362.

[24] Reginald Garrigou-Lagrange, *De Revelatione* (Rome, Casa Editrice Marietti, 1944), vol. I, p. 159: "*Ex parte causae materialis seu subjecti in quo recipitur Revelatio dividitur in* immediatam et mediatam. *Immediata est quae a recipitur a propheta, mediata autem quae mediante Propheta seu Ecclesia recipitur ab aliis fidelibus.*"

derived its meaning through relation to the rest of their existence. If the words of Christ were the pure, unmediated revelation, we would have to conclude that the apostles were grossly negligent in preserving the revelation, since we have practically no certain quotations from Christ. But we would be forced to interpret the variations within the apostolic testimony as various degrees of corruption only if revelation were conceived to be the words, ideas, and judgments placed immediately in the prophet or apostle.[25]

Secondly, there is a very important sense in which every Christian receives (or takes part in) revelation immediately; that is, he receives it not from men or books but from the in-dwelling Spirit. The definite part that holy Scripture, Church doctrine, official teachers, and other believing Christians play is a large one and we shall look to these shortly. What I wish to oppose here, nevertheless, is the supposition that revelation can be something outside man, something which can be passed down over the centuries, something which can be delivered to man by other men. God reveals and man believes; there is no revelation unless God is now acting and unless a human consciousness is now responding. For the individual believer revelation must happen in the present experience of the community; to this extent revelation must be immediate. The Catholic takes part in

[25] Oscar Cullmann, "Scripture and Tradition," in *Christianity Divided,* edited by Daniel Callahan, *et al.* (New York, Sheed and Ward, 1961), p. 16: "There is also this human element in the apostolic writings them-selves, which are also a transposing of the divine Word into human lan-guage. But behind them are the Apostles, the eyewitnesses. The human ele-ment is here reduced to an inevitable minimum inherent in the very notion of a divine Revelation to man." I would agree that the Christian under-standing must always be rooted in the apostolic testimony; but behind the apostles stands Christ who received God's Word not with the minimum of human receptiveness but with the maximum. The Scriptures and Church teachings are not human accretions to a pure Word received by the apostles; they are testimonies, insights and pointers to the Word received by the man Jesus. In this conception of revelation, it cannot be assumed that the human element is always corruptive, nor can it be assumed that the ideal is to have as little of the human element as possible.

this revelation through the help of the apostolic preaching as preserved in the Church; but it is God in Christ whom the Church is always teaching and believing in.[26]

We may conclude that there is a valid basis for distinguishing the role of prophet or apostle and that of the present-day Christian in the revelational history. However, the simplistic way in which theology books have often opposed mediate and immediate revelation makes of this an inadequate distinction. On both sides of the distinction there is a reduction of revelation to an impersonal thing, and there is complete neglect of the mysterious intercourse of divine and human which is the very heart of Christian revelation. It may be possible to salvage the terminology, but only if the whole revelational process is rethought so that the words can be better used and understood.

In summary, we have reaffirmed our earlier position that revelation is a personal union in knowledge between God and a participating subject in the revelational history of a community. While we may applaud the reaction against the notion of faith as a "holding of true doctrines," there is serious danger of replacing it with something no better or even something worse unless the full depths of the revelation question are reached. In particular, I have asserted that so long as knowledge is equated with the explicit judgments of the mind there will be an inorganic and external relation between revelation and life. When this is followed by a reaction which attempts to place revelation in a realm other than knowledge or beyond knowledge, the problem is only exacerbated. The only solution lies in overcoming the superficial understanding of knowledge that is the cause of the problem. As I have indicated, neither the Bible, nor contemporary philosophy and psychology, nor a genuine Thomistic philosophy, has such a superficial conception

[26] See Jean Mouroux, *I Believe* (New York, Sheed and Ward, 1959), p. 26: "No matter what the human intermediaries may be, it is the living and personal Word of God which presents the truth of faith to the soul until the end of time."

of knowledge. Unfortunately, this is not true of the most common presentations of revelation. The very fact that revelation is not examined at length and in depth practically guarantees that a superficial, common-sense notion of knowledge will be assumed and taught.

I have tried to show in this chapter that the knowledge which is revelation is well exemplified by the apostles' revelatory experience. Opening themselves to the work of the Spirit, they were transformed by the knowledge of Christ Jesus. Despite their lack of conceptual tools for explication of this knowledge, it is they who are first among Christians in the possession of Christian truth. What is needed among us their descendants, is not less emphasis on knowledge in favor of something else, but, on the contrary, more knowledge, deeper knowledge, and knowledge more suited to the subject who must open himself to it and participate in it. In that knowledge is eternal life.

V.

The Literary Objectification
of Revelation

THROUGHOUT the history of Christianity there has always been recognized an intimate connection between revelation and holy Scripture. What the precise relationship of these two is, however, has always been the subject of some debate. It is a well known fact that Protestant insistence upon the centrality of Scripture has sharpened the issue in recent centuries. Superficially, it has sometimes appeared that the difference between Protestantism and Catholicism resided in the former's acceptance of "Scripture alone" as the source of God's revelation and the latter's averment that revelation is also contained in tradition. The writing in recent years has shown that this formulation, while not entirely false, does not express very well the real issue. Divergent streams of thought have been uncovered within the supposedly simple opposition of Catholics and Protestants on this point. On the one hand, there is a strong current of Protestant writing which states that there must be clear distinction made between revelation and Scripture. There is thus often acknowledged the need for a continuing Church tradition. On the other hand, it is commonly held among Catholic theologians today that all revelation is in some way contained in holy Scripture.[1]

[1] See Baillie, *op. cit.,* pp. 109–110; McDonald, *op. cit.,* p. 161; Congar, *op. cit.,* pp. 79–119; Moran, *op. cit.,* pp. 29–45, 63–76.

This recent writing does not signify a *rapprochement* of Catholic and Protestant positions (or a reversal of positions), but it does hold out the possibility of greater understanding and the elimination of some pseudo-problems. The achievement of mutual understanding, however, demands that both Catholic and Protestant examine carefully the role which the Bible has for him in the process of Christian revelation. I should like in this chapter to determine: 1) whether the Bible is only a record of revelation or is in some sense revelation itself; 2) whether the Bible contains the whole revelation; 3) whether the Bible contains its own principles of interpretation.

THE WORD OF GOD

In the latter part of the Old Testament there was a tendency to embody "God's word" in a book which could then be consulted as a normative authority. In the post-exilic period this intellectualized version of revelation seemed to equate God's word with the law. This conception of word stood in some contrast to the earlier tradition that we have considered.[2] The New Testament revelation is more closely allied to that earlier tradition than to the more static conception of revelation in post-exilic times. Once the Word had been made flesh, there could no longer be question of reducing God's revelation to static categories of law depositable in a book. This being true, however, the development of the New Testament writings and references to these writings as the "word of God," might make it appear that Christianity had fallen into just such an error.

In the strictest meaning of the term there can be only one "Word of God," namely, the Word spoken by the Father from eternity, appearing on earth personally and in flesh at one historical time. As revelatory of the Father this Word was received and understood in the humanity of Jesus Christ. It is

[2] See Benoit, "Révélation et . . . , *loc. cit.,* p. 339; Jacob, *op. cit.,* p. 133.

96

possible, however, to extend the use of the phrase "word of God" beyond his person. It is clear, for example, that the physical words which Jesus spoke are in some sense words of God (Jn. 3:34). They are not identical with his person and yet they are not wholly distinct from him. The words which any person uses are not arbitrary signs standing for concepts. Words are symbols which do not stand wholly outside the reality symbolized. Words are the media of interpersonal communion in which knowledge is both expressed and formed. The words which Christ used, the style of speech, the choice of imagery and analogy, were not separable from "divine and eternal truths" simply placed in the words. The direct awareness of God in the human understanding of Christ became truly human knowledge only when it was brought to light by human words. The word which was spoken from the lips of Christ, therefore, was neither simply a word about God, nor was it simply the word of God. It was rather the objective element within a revelational process which because it includes man as a participant must include an objectifying moment.

By sharing in this divine-human knowledge which Christ possessed, the apostles also spoke words which were neither words about God nor words dictated by God. The apostles made no claim to be wise men discoursing on God. Their claim was much simpler and much more startling. They claimed to speak *in* Christ, to have been given the Spirit which enabled them to speak from within the mystery of God. Their words were put forth not as human words on a divine truth, but as words which could bring the believer face to face with Christ (Gal. 3:1) and convey to the believer a share in the wisdom proper to the Son (Phil. 2:5). The word that issued from this life in Christ and the word that mediated this knowledge of Christ was thus also spoken of as the "word of God."

Going one step further, we may say that the fixing of the gospel in written form did not alter its character as "word of

God." A written word may simply record a spoken word, or it may serve functions that the spoken word cannot. Although oral transmission of stories and teachings was a highly developed art among ancient peoples, the written word was obviously of advantage in preserving intact the apostolic teaching. Very early in the history of the Church the catechetical and liturgical missions gave impetus to fixing the apostolic preaching in definite patterns and written selections. As it became apparent that the Church was to continue after the apostolic age, these writings were collected into the book we call the New Testament. This New Testament writing, which was capable of bringing the mind into conformity with the mind of Christ, was also called the "word of God." If the Word that is God was to come to all men, then there had to be such a process in which preached and written words would mediate belief in the risen Lord.

The word has this peculiar character in human life: it is the way in which one person can deeply affect another without doing violence to his freedom. It is also the way in which a person commits his freedom. Until the word is spoken the personal engagement is not total. The word is thus a high point of human symbolism, while at the same time rising above all images to the infinite.[3] The word points below and above itself not because of its emptiness but because of its wealth of meaning. The word originates out of the depths of man's pre-conscious bodily presence in the world and carries within itself an intrinsic reference to an end beyond itself. All of this which is true of the word on a natural level is *a fortiori* true of the apostles' invitation to share in their belief objectified in the biblical testimony. The word which is always needed to make fully intelligible the symbols of man's life is of even more crucial importance when there is question of a supernatural reality being revealed through the medium of the natural.[4]

[3] See Rahner, "Priest and . . ." *loc. cit.*, p. 10.
[4] See Schillebeeckx, *Christ the . . .* , p. 99.

In attempting to convey the "mystery," that is, the person of Christ and man's relation to Christ in the plan of the Father, the apostles were forced to strain the capacities of their language and to create images which indirectly expressed but never fully expressed what they desired to say. It would be inaccurate to conceive of this language as either mere covering which can be stripped off to reveal the "truths" contained there or as empty markers which stand for a reality but do not convey any truth. The sensible and verbal images are never neutral or expendable; they unfold the mystery more deeply or else they distort it. The biblical language must be appreciated and understood within its full human context; it cannot be converted into "rational truths" which supposedly express the same thing in more scientific language.[5]

An aspect of this objectification through word which had not been emphasized until recently is the social nature of the entire process. The Bible is not only the objectification of the apostle's (or prophet's) teaching. It is something that emerged out of the life and work of the community. Modern study of the Bible has made it clear that the Old Testament grew out of the life and traditions of the Israelite people. The traditions recorded in the Old Testament antedate the written text. Many hands over a period of many years have usually joined in bringing to completion the established text.[6]

We should not generalize too hastily on this point; the Old Testament with its various kinds of literature does not allow easy generalizations. We cannot simply say that the Old Testament was written by the community; the stamp of individual genius and personal idiosyncrasy is too striking in many places. Nevertheless, even the individual prophet or historian who

[5] See Lonergan, op. cit., p. 548; Edmund Hill, "Remythologizing: the Key to Scripture," in Scripture, XVI (July, 1964), pp. 65–75.

[6] See McCarthy, loc. cit., pp. 554–561; John L. McKenzie, "The Social Character of Inspiration," in Catholic Biblical Quarterly, XXIV (April, 1962), pp. 116–120.

molded his material according to his own style was aware that he was working from within a tradition and that his work was turned toward the tradition.[7] Without denying the individual's contribution, therefore, we can still consider the Israelite nation as the subject of Old Testament writings. It was in the history of the Jewish people that God expressed himself symbolically.

It is important to note that just as on the level of the individual where language is not only expressive of thought but in turn helps to shape the thought, the same is true on the level of community, nation, or culture. Revelation is not only recorded in the Bible; to some degree the oral and written expression of it helped to create and to form the community experience. The Old Testament was not intended to be preserved only as a recounting of past events. The texts existed to be read by the community of the present; they conveyed an understanding of the present by recalling the past and holding out an ideal for the future. The Old Testament, first as oral tradition and then as national literary symbol, was both the effect and the cause of revelation. It originated from the community and was in turn formative of the community. Precisely because there was as yet no definitive norm, the reciprocal causal interplay of communal revelatory experience and individual-communal expression could continue throughout the whole of the Old Testament period.[8]

These considerations of the Old Testament have parallels in the New Testament writing, though, of course, there are important differences. The New Testament composition involves a far shorter period of time. There would be nothing comparable to the redaction which synthesized the traditions of the Pentateuch. Nevertheless, there was in the New Testament writing

---

[7] See Levie, *op. cit.*, p. 206; Carroll Stuhlmueller, "The Influence of Oral Tradition upon Exegesis," in *Catholic Biblical Quarterly*, XX (July, 1958), pp. 299–326.

[8] See McCarthy, *loc. cit.*, p. 574.

an interplay of individual and communal experience, a reciprocal relationship between lived knowledge and written expression. What was committed to writing was not the isolated formulations of an apostle but the preached and lived doctrine of the apostolic community. The apostles' experience of the Spirit, their own reflection upon the actions and words of Jesus, and all of their own external activity took place in the Church community. As with the Old Testament, the individual hagiographer contributed his own style and knowledge, but the ecclesial nature of nearly all parts of the New Testament writing is evident.[9]

The early chapters of the Acts of the Apostles show in striking fashion the deep communal sense possessed by the Church of the apostolic period. "The writings of the New Testament originate as life processes of the Church. They are the embodiment of that which in her has been transmitted and preached as her faith; they are writings which came into existence as manifestations of communal life."[10] This literary precipitate was one of the elements willed by God in the constitution of the Church's structure. As was true of the Old Testament, this very expression of the Church's faith in written form, especially for liturgical and catechetical purposes, was an element in the continuing revelation. By the forming of the Scriptures the Church was establishing herself as norm for future ages, while at the same time it was the very addressing of herself to future ages that helped to form the written expression of her belief.[11]

These considerations of the personal, historical, and social character of revelation help to clarify some of the recent writing

[9] See Rahner, *Inspiration in the Bible,* pp. 42–50; this does not deny the special role of the apostle in this process, as Yves Congar insists in "Inspiration des Ecritures canoniques et apostolicité de l'Eglise," in *Revue des sciences philosophiques et théologiques,* XLV (1961), pp. 32–42.

[10] Rahner, *Inspiration in the Bible,* p. 49. See *Constitution on Divine Revelation,* Chapter II, Article 7.

[11] *Ibid.,* pp. 49–50; J. Coppens, "Comment mieux concevoir et énoncer l'inspiration et l'inerrance des Saintes Ecritures," in *Nouvelle revue théologique,* XCVI (October, 1964), p. 946.

101

on the nature of inspiration. Earlier attempts to define inspiration were often hampered by rigid distinctions between intellectual and volitional elements, and by the assumption that authorship should and could be established on the same basis as modern day writing. Involved, too, were assumptions about revelation and its relation to the biblical text.

It was thought to be a great gain when inspiration and revelation were carefully separated from one another. It was emphasized that all parts of the Bible are inspired but that many parts of the Bible do not contain any revelation. Theological manuals were thus able to distinguish clearly between the "word of God," the revelation which the prophet or apostle was conscious of passively receiving from God; and the "action of God directed primarily to the writing of a book," the inspiration which moved the sacred writer to write without his necessarily being aware of God's direction.[12] What was wrong with this clear distinction was that there is neither much support for it in the Bible, nor does it fit the whole complex process as far as we can understand it.

It is impossible here to consider all the various aspects of the question of inspiration. I would like to cite, however, a few tendencies in recent writing that seem closely related to the understanding of revelation we are trying to develop. The understanding of revelation as a truly interpersonal reality is necessary in this area or else theories of inspiration will simply be adjusted *ad hoc* as successive difficulties arise. At present, several points have been discussed that hold out the possibility of deepening our understanding here.

Revelation and inspiration are not so easily separated as the previously quoted definitions would seem to imply. One can make a distinction between them, but one cannot make them successive steps in a series. They are elements of a single process

12 See Michael Nicolau and Joachim Salaverri, *Sacrae Theologiae* (3rd ed.; Matriti, Biblioteca de Autores Cristianos, 1955), p. 94.

which is both social and historical. "It seems to me," writes John L. McKenzie, "that the distinction between inspiration and revelation is based on an inadequate conception of both. . . . Inspiration has been too closely identified with the individual author and the written word; revelation has been too simply understood as a revealed proposition, and not as the word of God and the knowledge of God in the biblical sense."[13]

Inspiration, therefore, applies to much more than the writing of a book. It cannot be limited to the impulse of will supplied to an isolated writer. Inspiration in the widest sense is the directive action of God's providence as it envelops the history of God's people. From the community of Israel and from the early Christian Church there issued as a constituent element of their Spirit-directed lives an inspired literary expression. "For a comprehensive understanding of divine inspiration," as David Stanley says in this connection, "we must consider the effects of this charism not only upon the written or oral sources, the various redactors and glossators of the sacred books, but upon the entire ambient culture in which God's activity had worked for generations as an energizing leaven."[14] To the degree that writers in Israel and the Church were aware of the role they were playing in embodying this tradition in writing, scriptural inspiration would not be a wholly unconscious process.[15]

With inspiration conceived along these lines, exegetes are freed from a naïve conception of revelation as the passive reception of images and ideas. Revelation does concern knowledge, but a knowledge that is personal, historical, and social, that arose out of the community's experience before God. This knowledge was made more explicit by the reflection upon the life

[13] See McKenzie, "The Social . . . ," loc. cit., p. 122; Benoit, "Révélation et . . . ," loc. cit., p. 349; Levie, op. cit., pp. 204–205.

[14] See David Stanley, "The Concept of Biblical Inspiration," in Proceedings: Catholic Theological Society of America, XIII (1958), p. 70; C. Charlier, "Méthode historique et lecture spirituelle des Ecritures," in Bible et vie chrétienne, XVIII (1957), p. 16.

[15] See Rahner, Inspiration in the Bible, p. 63.

103

of the community, and in turn the knowledge helped to direct the community.

With this understanding of the historical and social dimensions of both revelation and inspiration, exegetical questions such as the "fuller sense" of Scripture are provided with a better background. There has been a long controversy over this sense of Scripture "intended by God but not clearly intended by the human author."[16] Although on the surface there remains a sharp disagreement between leading exegetes, there is in fact a strong consensus on the important things to be emphasized today. Viewing this question from outside Catholic theology, Robinson surmised that "the *aggiornamento* wing of *sensus plenior* and those who reject it in favor of the protection of the *sensus litteralis* may tend to merge."[17] One would hesitate to say that the controversy has become mostly an academic question with little practical importance except that this has in fact been admitted by figures on both sides of the question.[18] I have no intention here of trying to redefine or unravel the question; I wish simply to indicate that a better understanding of the revelation-inspiration process would be of great help in clarifying an issue such as this.[19]

Discussion here has often been hampered by the supposition,

[16] For this definition of the "fuller sense" of Scripture, see Raymond Brown, *The* Sensus Plenior *of Sacred Scripture* (Baltimore, St. Mary's University, 1955), p. 92. This work together with the same author's article, "The *Sensus Plenior* in the Last Ten Years," in *Catholic Biblical Quarterly*, XXV (October, 1963), pp. 262–285, is the best English summary of the case for the fuller sense of Scripture; see also Pierre Benoit, "La plénitude de sens des livres saints," *Revue biblique*, LXVII (1960), pp. 161–196.

[17] James M. Robinson, "Scripture and Theological Method," in *Catholic Biblical Quarterly*, XXVII (January, 1965), p. 22.

[18] See Brown, "The *Sensus Plenior* in the Last Ten Years," *loc. cit.*, p. 281; Bruce Vawter, "The Fuller Sense: Some Considerations," in *Catholic Biblical Quarterly*, (January, 1964), p. 85.

[19] This tendency to place the question against such a broader background seems indicated in recent articles, such as Benoit, "Révélation et Inspiration," *loc. cit.*; Coppens, "Comment mieux concevoir . . . ," *loc. cit.*; N. Lohfink, "Über die Irrtumslösigkeit und die Einheit der Schrift," in *Stimmen der Zeit*, CLXXIV (1964), pp. 161–181.

104

made by both supporters and opponents of a "fuller sense," that a statement contains a truth proper to it, that a "meaning" can be fairly easily isolated and defined. The question then becomes whether another level of meaning might be conveyed through the statement, a meaning of which the human author might be unconscious, marginally conscious, or indirectly conscious.[20] Authors on both sides have come to see that the discussion is vitiated by a not sufficiently deep understanding of truth, symbolism, meaning, and language. These questions need not be resolved before there is any agreement, but a better understanding of these questions would keep the arguments from becoming only verbal.

If we take seriously the thoroughly personal, historical, and social nature of revelation and inspiration, this should provide a wider base of agreement from which to work. The development of understanding within the Old Testament, developments in New Testament times, and the fulfillment of the Old Testament in the New, can be appreciated without violating the requirements of scientific exegesis. That scientific control of the text would be endangered by the admission of a "fuller sense" is no doubt possible, but the danger seems remote when in practice good exegetes, whether supporters or opponents of the "fuller sense," go about their work in the same way. It may be, however, that it is not in the best use of words to speak of a "fuller sense" of a single text. Perhaps it would be more accurate to speak of a "fuller understanding" coming through later developments.[21] But this distinction would have to be based

---

[20] On whether the fuller sense requires some consciousness on the part of the author, see Brown, "The *Sensus Plenior* in the Last Ten Years," *loc. cit.,* p. 267; Charlier, *loc. cit.,* pp. 25–26; J. Coppens, *Le problème du sens plénier des Saintes Ecritures* (Bruges, Desclée de Brouwer, 1957), p. 16.

[21] For the preference of a "fuller understanding of Scripture" as opposed to a fuller meaning of a text, see Vawter, "The Fuller Sense . . . ," *loc. cit.,* p. 92; John L. McKenzie, "The Continuing Dialogue; letter to the editor," in *Theology Digest,* IX (Spring, 1961), p. 66; see also Robinson, "Scripture and . . . ," *loc. cit.,* p. 20.

upon philosophical and theological analysis as much as on exegetical arguments.

In any case it would be profitable to examine at greater length the relation between revelation and its inspired objectification in testifying word by individuals within and for a community. The expressed judgment is a necessary but always incomplete objectification of man's experience of the revealing God, the objective expression helping to complete the experience while at the same time pointing beyond itself. It would seem that a better understanding of this process would overcome some of the apparent dichotomies. It should then be possible to preserve the scientific exegesis of texts and at the same time give full value to the developmental character of Scripture, to preserve the gains from giving primacy to the literal sense and at the same time to trace various themes throughout the Bible, and to give legitimacy and truth value to statements in the Old Testament while also seeing their fulfillment in Christ. Whether the term "fuller sense" will survive and be useful or whether it will be absorbed into a better classification is another question. The answer to that question will probably come less from arguing over the term and definitions and more from developments in biblical theology and revelation-inspiration theory.

THE CONTENT OF SCRIPTURE

Within the wider context of the revelational process we have described, we may now raise the question whether or not all revelation is contained in holy Scripture. The immediate answer might seem to be that no revelation is contained in Scripture, at least according to any ordinary meaning that we give to the word "contain." Although it is possible to redefine words to suit one's purpose, the formulation of the question "Is all revelation contained in Scripture?" seems to be unfortunate and to be predisposed to ambiguity and confusion.

When statements of logic and mathematics are at issue there

is some justification for speaking of the truth contained in the statements. The accuracy of these rests upon the precision with which each term is defined and used. But the use of language in mathematics and logic is not the prototype for all use of language. "Over against this language that says all that can be said is the language that says nothing of what can be said, or almost nothing—the language of intimacy where innuendo predominates, where each word indicates an attitude and evokes a possibility of interior adventure."[22]

Human affairs are not reducible to logical, mathematical, and scientifically empirical statements. In the ordinary judgments on the real order and especially in the exchange of personal knowledge and love, words are intended to open out on life and communicate more than could ever be put in words. The entire human context of a statement gives it a meaning which no amount of logical analysis can demonstrate. "The proposition is always a kind of window through which a view may be gained of the thing itself, and implies in its full sense (as Communication) this view of the thing through proposition (in its 'stated' sense)."[23]

Since this is true on the level of ordinary human discourse, it should be clear that the Bible communicates more than it states, that its statements point to realities which go beyond all possible statements. If revelation is the communication of a divine reality within human experience, no human statements can exhaust the reality of that revelation. Every person defies all attempts to summarize him; *a fortiori* is this true of the God-man and his experience. The evangelist John was speaking literally when he said that all the books in the world would not be sufficient for describing the person and activities of the Saviour (Jn. 21:25).

[22] Gusdorf, *op. cit.,* p. 66.
[23] Rahner, "Development of . . . ," *loc. cit.,* p. 69; see also Edward Dhanis, "Révélation explicite et implicite," in *Gregorianum,* XXXIV (April, 1953), pp. 186–237.

Nothing but an inveterate rationalism could make us be surprised that the Bible is not a unified scientific treatise of "revealed doctrines." What is true of everything deeply human was preëminently true of the revelation to Christ and his apostles: it could not be stated; it could only be witnessed to. Revelation could not be put in a book; it takes place in the experience of people who give witness to it with their lives. The revelation to the apostles thus transcended the human capacity to conceptualize, judge, and explain. When it came time to testify in writing to its experience, the apostolic community through the mediation of individual writers expressed itself in the testimonies of faith that we call the New Testament. The Church could later recognize these books as her own even without external proofs, for the Scriptures were the objectification of the Church's self-understanding.[24]

The scriptural testimony which the Church fixed in the process of becoming the norm for all future ages of the Church is itself the written, objective norm beyond which and outside of which the Church can never go. This is not to say, however, that Christian revelation is nothing but what is in the book, for the book is the written norm that both reflects the Church's life and helps to deepen it. "The true greatness of Holy Scripture," writes Levie, "is not that it is something final; that which is final is the Church growing into the fullness of Christ. The true greatness of Holy Scripture is that it is a starting point, an immovable foundation with which the Church must always remain in contact."[25]

[24] See Rahner, *Inspiration in the Bible*, p. 25. This involves the canonicity problem or the question of how the Church recognized which books are inspired. Rahner's analogy of the Church's "I consciousness" seems to be the most helpful image in understanding the Church's recognition of the inspired books. B. Brinkmann, while largely agreeing with Rahner, differs in holding that the Church chose (on the basis of revelation) which books to include in the canon without necessarily being exhaustive; see B. Brinkmann, "Inspiration und Kanonizität der Hl. Schrift in ihrem Verhältnis zur Kirche," in *Scholastik*, XXIII (April, 1958), pp. 229–231.

[25] Levie, *op. cit.*, p. 278.

The Church could not wait for the texts of holy Scripture to be written. The Church began by living. Out of that life scriptural texts emerged and back to that life the texts pointed. In forming the canon and in passing on the books of Scripture, the Church did set a definitive norm for herself; but it was precisely because there was a *Church* that there was a norm. The purpose of the New Testament writing was to express, to reflect, and to deepen the communal life in the Spirit; and the purpose of the canon was to guarantee that this "more than written reality" would continue.

The question of the Catholic doctrine of tradition, therefore, is not whether all the truths of revelation were committed to a book which binds the Church. The question is whether what God has given to man goes beyond all written or oral expression. What is handed over in the Church is the Church. This is what is fundamental to the notion of tradition.[26] One should not stop with this meaning of tradition but one must start here if definitions of different kinds of tradition are not to become hopelessly confused as has happened not only at Trent but in recent writing as well. Holy Scripture grew out of the Church's tradition and it helps to mold that continuing life in every era. In the context of her whole tradition the Bible is read and understood by the believing Church. The Church reflects upon her own life as it is verbally mediated to her by the words of holy Scripture. The Scripture as the verbal precipitate of her tradition is always at the base of her meditation and self-understanding.[27]

The whole of God's revelation, therefore, is reflected in the scriptural testimony. This is but another way of saying that the New Testament is the written testimony of the apostolic Church to God's revelation in Jesus Christ. Given the present under-

[26] See *Constitution on Divine Revelation,* Chapter II, Article 8.

[27] On this point with reference to the Church's definition of the dogma of the assumption, see *AAS,* XLII (1950), p. 767; see also *Constitution on Divine Revelation,* Chapter VI, Article 21.

standing of holy Scripture and revelation, the assertion that Scripture contains only part of revelation must be judged not incorrect but unintelligible.

The controversy formulated in terms of the "one-source theory" or the "two-source theory" was not entirely to the point. This was so not only because the word "source" was ill-defined, but because there was a difference of attitudes not sufficiently exposed in most of the argumentation.[28] Those who claimed to be defending a "second source" were usually not aware that what was at issue was not the place of tradition but their own conception of revelation. The Second Vatican Council has now situated holy Scripture and sacred tradition not as "sources" but as the "mirror" in which the believing Church beholds God revealing.[29] The rethinking of the revelational process has undercut the Scripture-tradition question and focused upon the underlying differences.

Understanding Scripture

For grasping the meaning of revelation through holy Scripture, the Church cannot be content with grammatical and linguistic tools alone even though these are indispensable. An individual text must be situated within a particular form of writing and

---

[28] In my *Scripture and Tradition,* I tried to show that there were two distinct meanings of the word "source" that were constantly being confused; this clarification of terms, I maintained, was necessary if any fruitful argument was to take place. Tavard, *loc. cit.,* p. 450, criticized this "optimism" by saying: "Once a concordance has been established between the terms and their uses, there remains the more profound question of why a certain theology tends to seek expression in one way, whereas another falls, as it were spontaneously, into an altogether different semantic universe." I would agree entirely with this and have expressed the same idea in "Scripture-Tradition . . . ," *loc. cit.,* p. 353.

[29] See *Constitution on Divine Revelation,* Chapter II, Article 7: "*Haec igitur Sacra Traditio et utriusque Testamenti Scriptura veluti speculum sunt in quo Ecclesia in terris peregrinans contemplatur Deum, a quo omnia accipit, usquedum ad Eum videndum facie ad faciem sicuti est perducatur.*"

this in turn viewed against the larger pattern of a complete work or a writer's synthesis. Ultimately, the Church accepts a harmony of the whole Bible stemming from its inspiration by God and its unity of testimony to the one revelation of God to man. The criterion which the Church uses for understanding parts of the Bible is the whole Bible; this is her "principle of Catholicity."[30] It is no doubt easier to base one's theology upon selected parts of holy Scripture, but the nature of revelation and its partial objectification by an historical community means that one must seek the whole revelation in the whole Bible. We are not, however, prevented from saying that every expression of Scripture (even brief "occasional writings") can open out upon the fullness of revelation provided that it be viewed within the whole and that no meaning be in principle excluded. In this case the Church's tradition would still be the implicit context for the believer's understanding of holy Scripture.[31]

I would insist still further that the principle of the whole does not only mean a gathering together and examining of all the texts presumably by scholarly exegetes. The whole, the ultimate norm for the Church, is Jesus Christ, who is first revealed not in the written records but in the thought of Jesus Christ. The Church accepts the scriptural canon as normative for her teaching, but Scripture itself points beyond itself to the revelation accepted by Christ and shared in by the apostolic community. The Church cannot find Jesus unless she reads the Scriptures, but it is Jesus she seeks when she reads. He is the final principle of unity and integrity, and not someone's school of exegesis or someone's biblical theology. If the apostles had been the original source to whom revelation was given, we should have understood revelation simply by a scholarly study of the thought-patterns of the apostles as expressed in their writings. But the apostles do not share with us the knowledge

---

[30] See Küng, *Structures of the Church,* p. 164.
[31] See *Constitution on Divine Revelation,* Chapter III, Article 12.

which belonged to them; we and the apostles together share in a knowledge which transcends both of us. The purpose of the apostolic writings is to lead us beyond apostle and writing to the mind of Christ.[32]

Revelation cannot be confined to any text; revelation happens in the living experience of men. The words of holy Scripture passed down to us from the apostles represent one aspect of the revelational process. These words, as I have said, are not just a record of a prior revelatory event; these words are intrinsic to the revelational process and help to constitute it. As the objective expression of revelation these words exercise an inner guidance in the revelational experience which continues in the post-apostolic Church. It should be obvious that if the text of Scripture is to be revelatory of God, it has to be read (or heard), understood, and appreciated. The scriptural words are an invitation by the apostles to enter with them into the mind of Christ. When the later Christian accepts these words as his own, they become not only the testimony of the apostles to their experience, but the expression of the believer's life as well. Each generation of men must make these words its own as the ever valid rule of men's lives in that generation.[33]

The believer must read Scripture with the same attitude with which it was written, that is, as the expression of a believing individual within the Church. The biblical writing was originally intended and still is primarily intended to give Christians a deeper understanding of what they already believe. The mind of the believer should already be in harmony with the general structure of revelation; only to the mind living in the conditions of the covenant does Scripture surrender its meaning. The reader of Scripture as well as the writer receives the word in faith with the guidance of the Spirit and the direction of the Church's understanding. The divine help that was given to the Church

---

[32] See Levie, *op. cit.*, p. 210.
[33] See Rahner, "Development of . . . ," *loc. cit.*, p. 68.

which resulted in the writing of Scripture means, too, that it will always be the Church which reads this book and has divine guidance in understanding it. The individual believer participates in this reading of the Bible by the Church, and, as Levie says, "the nearer he is to Christ in the Church through his whole supernatural life, through his enlightened faith and his efforts toward holiness, the better he is able to perceive the profound religious riches of Scripture."[34]

Any attempt to go beyond the message of Scripture in the sense of adding new "revealed truths" to the norm of the apostolic Church is rejected by Catholic belief. The ordinary personal experience of the Christian must be constantly measured for its truth against the Church's objective norm. The same holds true of extraordinary religious experience, that is, "private revelations." These, too, must be measured by the revelation made complete in Jesus Christ and testified to in holy Scripture. Such "revelations" cannot add to the truth of the gospel, but they are intended (presuming they are authentic) to direct the gospel to the particular needs of the day.[35] On these principles it would be possible to connect "private revelations" more closely to the ordinary Christian life. They would simply be the continuing Christian revelation brought to an intense awareness in relation to some need of the age. All extraordinary phenomena need not be excluded, but such phenomena are not what is essential in "private revelations."

Finally, we may relate what we have said here to the historical character of revelation as discussed in Chapter 2. The New

[34] Levie, *op. cit.,* p. 248.

[35] See J. H. Nicolas, "Le foi et les signes," in *Supplément de la vie spirituelle,* XXV (May, 1953), p. 158; Laurent Volken, *Visions, Revelations and the Church* (New York, P. J. Kenedy and Sons, 1963), p. 224; Karl Rahner, *Visions and Prophecies* (New York, Herder and Herder, 1963), p. 106. All refer to St. Thomas's teaching on this point (*S.T.* IIa-IIae, q. 174, a. 6, ad 3); and also the remarks of Pope John on Lourdes, *AAS,* LI (1959), pp. 144, 147.

Testament even more clearly than the Old, is first tied not to
a pattern of facts and events but to people. Assuredly, these
are historical people, but the history emerges from the people
and not vice versa. For this reason, there is a wide variety of
literature used in testifying to God's revelation. For some modern people there may seem to be shockingly little "historical
writing" in the New Testament, but there is nevertheless plenty
of writing in the New Testament which gives insight into historical people.[36] Although every individual text may be called
into question as to the historical facts it recounts and how far
"facts" are therein overlaid with theology, the presupposition of
the whole work is that the people involved are historical people.

The early Church, while apparently uninterested in many details of Christ's earthly life, held dearly to her insights into his
person and the meaning of his life, death, and resurrection.
Christianity is not merely the recountal of an historical revelation in the past—as I shall show in the next chapter—but it
is inescapably tied to certain documents written in the past, concerning a person who lived on earth at one time and not any
other. The work of the exegete is to bring out the full meaning
of these documents and to investigate without hesitation or fear
the kinds and degrees of historical reporting used in the scriptural testimony to revelation. To the objection that once we start
finding literary forms in the *New Testament,* "where do we
stop?", Stanley replied: "We 'stop' when we have been satisfied
that we understand completely the words of the inspired writer,
since then we know we have grasped the divine message intended for us in the biblical passage."[37]

[36] See Brown, "After Bultmann . . . ," *loc. cit.,* pp. 6–8; Robinson, *A New
Quest . . . ,* pp. 89–90.
[37] David Stanley, "The Conception of our Gospels as Salvation History,"
Theological Studies, XX (December, 1959), p. 585, n. 77.

VI.

The Continuing Revelation
in the Church

THE revelation of God, as we have already said, reached its high point and fullness in the consciousness of the glorified Lord. According to Catholic belief, that person, Jesus Christ, continues to live in a new mode of time and in a higher kind of life. But if this is so, then revelation still continues to happen, that is, the Father still speaks the Word which resounds in the humanity of Christ and in the world united to Christ.

The New Testament presents the life of Christ as a journey in which Jesus, returning to the Father, passed from the bondage of flesh to the freedom of spirit through his death and resurrection. His journey found its completion in his reception into eternal glory.[1] God's plan for mankind unfolded wholly in Christ to whom all gifts were given. Other men are given not what the risen Christ lacks but what is given to him in superabundance. As the mediator who reveals God, Christ did not bring his work to an end with his death-resurrection; rather, it was then that it began in full effectiveness.

Entering into glory, Christ became the revelatory-redemptive principle of God's action with men of all future time. He re-

[1] S. Lyonnet, "La valeur sotériologique de la résurrection du Christ selon saint Paul," in *Christus Victor Mortis* (Rome, Pontificia Università Gregoriana, 1958), p. 113.

mains the one way that leads to the Father, eternally revealing God's love for us and offering man's worship to God.[2] The Letter to the Hebrews portrays Christ as our eternal high priest who has entered beyond the veil of the holy of holies and sits at the right hand of God. He is our ground of confidence, our sure access to the throne of God. God's revelation is meant for all men, but the unified, completed revelation cannot perdure in a book, an institution, or preaching; the salvation event is not in a message but in a person.[3]

Although it is frequently said in theological writing today that Christ is our heavenly high priest who still "acts" to save us, it is less often said that he also continues to reveal the Father. But these two, Revealer and Life-Giver, can never be entirely separated; they both pertain to the same mediatorial role. If Christ is not understood to be *now* revealing God to man, faith is bound to become (despite our protests to the contrary) the rational acceptance of past facts and present teachings which are extrinsic to the sanctifying-worshiping activity now taking place. But belief is not directed to a message but to God raising up Christ, and this is not a past event but an ever present, continuing occurrence.

THE CHURCH: PRESENT REVELATORY SIGN

The revelation-redemption took place in the body of the Saviour; only in him is it fully accomplished. Nevertheless, it was precisely as head of the human race, as ontologically bound to his brothers, that he became the first-born from the dead (Col. 1:18). All men are now called upon to ratify this redemption within their own lives by adhering to the risen Lord. Those who do follow him in faith, within the society he has formed, share in his knowledge and love of God. Thus we refer to these

[2] See Juan Alfaro, "Cristo glorioso, revelador del Padre," in *Christus Victor Mortis,* p. 66.

[3] See *Constitution on Divine Revelation,* Chapter I, Article 2.

people who make up his Church as the "Body of Christ." However, our terminology does not always make clear that the Church is a prolongation not primarily of the historical Christ but of the heavenly Christ. The Church does not only continue the good actions which Christ once performed on earth. She is rather the present sign and the partial fulfillment of the present revelatory-redemptive process.

The "mystery" for St. Paul included not only the preparatory plan and the death-resurrection of Christ, but also the fullness of his body and the revealing of his glory (1 Tim. 3:16). The chief sign of our redemption is the heavenly body of Christ; but "the Lord gave this external sign of the redemption a visible prolongation on earth: the visible Church. Through this visible prolongation the redemption is revealed in this world as something that is for us, and thus it is precisely through this that the redemption is offered to us."[4] The Church is never a mere formal framework, an institution in which men are molded for God. She is rather the yeas of the believers inspired by the Spirit in whom God continues to give himself ever anew to the knowledge and love of men. The Church must never confuse *herself* with God, nor can she claim to have fulfilled all of Christ's desires for her. Nevertheless, she does present herself—despite all her human weaknesses—as the focal point of God's revelation happening in the world and as the sign through which men can go to God.

This conception of the Church is implicit in the First Vatican Council's declarations on the role of the Church in faith. The characteristics of the Church which are there cited are not external props of the Church but belong to her essence. As that Council's *Constitution on the Faith* declares: "The Church itself, because of its marvelous propagation, its exalted sanctity, and its inexhaustible fruitfulness in all that is good, because of its catholic unity and its unshaken stability, is a great and perpetual motive of credibility and an irrefutable proof of its own

[4] Schillebeeckx, *Christ the . . . ,* p. 50.

divine mission."[5] Being herself the place of the concrete, continuing revelation, the Church exhibits the marks of revelation, especially in what are called miracle and prophecy.[6]

In the person of Christ the lines of prophecy and miracle came together and reached their definitive high point. God's redeeming presence in Christ means that miracle becomes the "natural" effect upon man's world and prophecy the "natural" effect upon man's history. The miracle of the resurrection is the beginning of the miraculous world order of which the Church is a striking sign among the nations. Insofar as the Church is living up to her mission, men are brought face to face with God through the extraordinary religious phenomenon of the Church's life.

In similar manner, the totalization of time that takes place in Christ's resurrection-ascension makes the eschatological event of prophecy an ever present occurrence. To the degree that the Church is capable of viewing the world processes in the light of Christ, the subject who sees and influences all history, prophecy is a normal part of the Church's life. The past, the present, and the future should take on a greater degree of intelligibility and provide the Christian with a better understanding of his own life. "Every baptized Christian, it might be inferred, is a 'prophet,' a receiver of revelation, by calling and status and inherent quality, in a way in which no Old Testament prophet could be."[7] The Christian is to experience the light of God's Word and God's Spirit and to speak in God's name.

A very important aspect of the Church's role is to bear and protect the deposit of faith. However, this needs to be viewed in relation to her over-all mission as the quasi-sacramental word in which grace becomes manifest in history and calls men to salvation. "She is, as divine mystery, herself the object of this

[5] Translation from Clarkson *et al.*, *The Church Teaches*, p. 30

[6] See Dumont, *loc. cit.*, p. 147.

[7] Victor White, "St. Thomas's Conception of Revelation," in *Dominican Studies*, I (January, 1948), p. 32.

118

revelation. She is at the same time the manner in which God's revelation and salvation are present to us. She is, to the extent that her inner nature is visible to us in the realm of historical experience, also the criterion of revelation."[8]

The time of the Church is the time of the continuing revelation in which the Church grows daily in her understanding of Christ. We seek to have the mind of Christ, but we remain far from it during our life on earth. We cannot get closer to this goal than did the apostles who ate and drank with the risen Lord. Thus the Church is indissolubly tied to the apostolic testimony as the unchanging deposit and the means that she must use to approach the mind of Christ while she remains on earth. It is not, however, a past revelation which she preserves; she lives in the present where revelatory-redemptive activity goes on, and she also looks to the future, to the time when the glory of the Lord will be revealed.

The almost exclusive concentration upon the past whenever revelation is discussed to any extent in Catholic works is most unfortunate. Repeatedly the statements are made: "Revelation is closed. All the necessary truths are known. There will never be any new truths imposed upon our faith." This is true, of course; there are no new "revealed truths" to be given, [no quantitative increase in the deposit]. But the clear assumption behind these statements is that revelation consists in a numerable collection of truths; and if there is no addition to this number, then revelation is something being preserved from the past.

The meaning of revelation is not exhausted by its "objective content." For this reason, revelation can be a continuing happening in our world today. *How* revelation continues is indeed a mystery, but no more so than the entire sacramental-moral life of Christianity which adds nothing to the "objective content" of Calvary. The Church's magisterium had earlier emphasized the objective side of revelation and the immutability of

8 Bulst, *op. cit.*, p. 123.

the deposit. The Second Vatican Council has now provided a wider and deeper perspective, beginning not with a certain number of truths, but with the self-communication of God to man. This self-donation of God obviously is not something that ceased with the apostolic age. It begins with fundamental newness in the life of each man and it continues in the community of the Church.

Revelation, therefore, is closed only in the sense in which a never to be surpassed high point has been reached which opens the revelation to all men. This high point is the "beginning of the infinite pouring out of Christ's fullness into that of the Church, of the Church's growth into the fullness of Christ and of God."[9] God has said all that he wished to say or could say in the Word of God. There is no going beyond the Word, no leaving him behind, as Joachim of Flora or other mystics may have hoped to do in expecting the "third age," the age of the Spirit.[10] The Spirit's age has indeed come, but it is the Word that the Spirit reveals in the continuing Pentecost. There is no increase of revelation, but there is a movement of the Spirit to conform the minds of the faithful to the mind of Christ where revelation continues in fullness. He has left us that he may come to us in the Spirit.

Revelation is not a thing, an object that can be placed somewhere and kept intact. Revelation is what happens between persons and exists only as a personal reality. If there is revelation anywhere in the Church today, it can only be in the conscious experience of people. Recent sacramental theology has brought out the point that Christ did not store up "grace" which is later distributed to those who fulfill certain requirements. In Christ's bodily humanity at the resurrection, the transformation by Spirit began in full; in Christ's body there has been nothing to stop it ever since then. In the Christian life of worship Christ's revelatory-redeeming activity brings the believer

[9] Urs von Balthasar, *Word and Revelation*, p. 29.
[10] Eliade, *op. cit.*, p. 145; Mersch, *op. cit.*, pp. 415–416.

into contact with the continuing event of salvation. The Word still speaks a word which like all human words is to a degree revelatory and effective, that is, effective because it is revelatory and revelatory because it is effective. But his word beyond all human words has a revelatory and effective (redeeming) power that reaches to the deepest resources of men's hearts.

THE LITURGY: SUMMIT OF CONTINUING REVELATION

The Church which is the prolongation of the heavenly high priest is both institution and event, or hierarchically structured community and symbolic activity of the community. To express what she is and to deepen what she has become, the Church performs activities that symbolize her life. These revelatory-sanctifying events call the Church's being more or less completely into act. I am particularly interested here in the activity which is meant to symbolize most perfectly her whole life, that is, the liturgical act. The Church community gathered for the liturgy is not simply a fragment of the Church universal; it is the whole Church concentrated, as it were, in miniature. The liturgy in act *is* the Church spatio-temporally realized.[11]

The liturgical assembly is called together to experience in faith God's revelation and to join in Christ's worshiping-sanctifying act. Because God has been revealed as a person, because Christ brought together the priestly and prophetic traditions, every Christian liturgical activity contains the worshipful gesture of the priestly and the revelatory word of the prophetic.[12] Within the Christian era every bodily gesture expressive of belief is a word of faith; conversely, every word of faith arises from and finds its completion in the personal experience which

[11] See I. H. Dalmais, *Introduction to the Liturgy* (Baltimore, Helicon, 1961), pp. 38–55; Karl Rahner, *The Church and the Sacraments* (New York, Herder and Herder, 1963), pp. 11-24.

[12] See Rahner, "Priesterliche Existenz," in *Schriften zur . . . ,* Band III, p. 292.

121

goes beyond words. These two, the verbal and the beyond-the-verbal, are indissolubly united in Christianity and *a fortiori* in the liturgy. Nevertheless, though the two are never separated, there can be a difference of emphasis and a distinction between elements. In considering the liturgy we can look first to reading and preaching and second to the sacrament.

The text of holy Scripture assumes its full revelatory *event value* as it is spoken aloud at the liturgical service. Revelation happens here and now because the word that is spoken is the inspired word of God; this is the word that is efficacious in uniting us to the mind of Christ. The proclaiming of the word of holy Scripture together with the reflection upon it by the minister is always a *hodie* making known or revealing what God is doing now. The minister, even if it be necessary for him to explain in detail the meaning of the Scripture, remains a servant and a witness to that living word of authority that has been transmitted from the apostles.[13] The minister's aim is always to bring about the understanding of God's invitation and a willing acceptance of his love and its demands. Undoubtedly, the minister must use different approaches to achieve this according to the situation and needs of his people. These approaches are distinct but not essentially different ways of presenting God's message.[14]

Although every reading of holy Scripture by a believer can mediate the revelatory action of God in his life, the liturgical assembly is the most proper milieu for this occurrence.[15] When Scripture is read by the individual believer the whole Church is implicitly there in him. What the liturgy does is bring to concreteness and explicitness the actual revelational structure.

[13] See Ratzinger, *Episcopate and Primacy*, p. 54.
[14] See P. A. Liégé, "Contenu et pédagogie de la prédication chrétienne," in *La Maison-Dieu*, XXXIX (1954), pp. 31–33.
[15] See Edward Schillebeeckx, "Revelation in Word and Deed," in *The Word*, p. 266.

In the liturgical reading the Christian community shares in knowledge with the apostolic community which wrote the Scripture. Here once again human words, which are in some sense divine words, are delivered by the prophetic leader of the community so that the whole congregation may be transformed by hearing the message. It is "a common search by preacher and hearers, praying together to the Holy Spirit, who alone gives understanding of the word."[16]

The experience of God's revealing and redeeming love does not pertain to isolated individuals but to a community of persons ever opening outward toward the inclusion of parish, diocese, church, and the world. The movement toward personal and world transformation is effected not only by the preacher's authoritative word and the congregation's acceptance, it is also helped by the testimony of each man to all the others. Every prayerful word, every word which is spoken in truth and charity, is an aid to the effectiveness of the scriptural word. "The charismatic gifts which Christians receive, and especially the inspired hymns (Eph. 5:19; Col. 3:16), make this knowledge of theirs deeper. And Paul often prays that their progress may grow without stopping, and that thus they may come to fullness of the perfect Christian."[17]

Throughout the whole of this eschatological era, God's revealing continues in the activity of his Church. The reading of and reflecting upon holy Scripture is a privileged instance of this revelatory activity. The liturgical reading of Scripture unveils even more clearly the God of love. The reading of holy Scripture, however, is still not the most complete expression of the revelational structure of Christianity. Words originate out of the pre-conceptual experience of human life and find their

[16] Jean Daniélou, "Parole de Dieu et mission de l'Eglise," in *Le prêtre, ministre de la parole* (Paris, Union des Oeuvres Catholiques de France, 1954), p. 49.
[17] Cerfaux, *op. cit.*, p. 416.

total meaning only when regrounded in personal existence as a whole. Man in his entire bodily self is to be taken up into God's revealing and redeeming love. "Faith comes by hearing," but this hearing is not only done with the ears. Man with all of his earthly capabilities and with the very core of his person must await and "hear."

Holy Scripture, sacred, revealing, salvific as it is, still only mediates the revelation verbally. Despite the fact that language is the symbol most proper to human existence, and despite the fact that holy Scripture sediments within itself the whole of revelation, words cannot be separated from symbols more bodily in character, else the words become flat, empty, and abstract. Holy Scripture of itself is thus oriented toward a bodily expression of revelation not because Scripture is an incomplete part of revelation, but because Scripture must be bodied forth in transforming man.[18]

At the end of the Middle Ages, an unfortunate dichotomy in the picture of man, together with a superficial and allegorized understanding of sacraments, had clouded the inner relation of word and person. This led the reformers to deëmphasize the sacrament ("a word for the unlettered") and concentrate on making intelligible the word of preaching. In this Reformation it was not the emphasis on holy Scripture and preaching that was regrettable, but the failure to carry the revelatory action beyond verbalization to a completion which Scripture itself indicates.[19]

[18] Schillebeeckx, "Revelation in . . . ," *loc. cit.,* p. 264; Urs von Balthasar, *Word and Revelation,* p. 15.

[19] See Bouyer, *Word, Church and Sacraments,* pp. 71–73; Cyril Richardson, "Word and Sacrament in Protestant Worship," in S. Miller and G. E. Wright (editors), *Ecumenical Dialogue at Harvard* (Cambridge, Harvard University, 1964), p. 155; Oscar Cullmann, *Early Christian Worship* (Chicago, Henry Regnery Co., 1953), pp. 30–31, pointed out the unity of Scripture readings and Lord's supper in the early documents of the Church; the same point is developed in Catholic writing in *Liturgy and the Word of God* (Collegeville, Liturgical Press, 1959).

Catholic writing, as well as Protestant writing, has been affected by these dichotomies even to the present day. Despite the constant assertion in recent writing that there is a close relation between liturgy of word and liturgy of sacrificial banquet, there still lurks the assumption that in the first part of the Mass man is "instructed in the revelation" and in the latter part he offers worship and is sanctified. What must be realized and thoroughly understood is that a liturgy of word is not only a speaking of revelation and a response of faith, but, that it is at the same time an act of worship and sanctification. Conversely, the liturgy of the eucharistic banquet and the liturgy of every sacrament is not only worshipful-sanctifying, but also revelatory of God and an affirmation of faith.

What is at issue here is not just terminology; there can be much flexibility in the way authors use words. But revelation and faith cannot be truly personal, social, and historical if we slip back into an implicit identification of revelation and Scripture, or revelation and the written or spoken word. Our conception of the relation between revelation and sacrament is a test case to determine whether we have freed revelation and faith from an impersonal way of thinking. Sacraments do not parallel or add to revelation; they *are* revelation. Sacraments are the intersubjective experience of the Christian community and God: God giving himself in Christ to man in community; and man receiving the gift in "active passivity," thereby rendering worship in and through Christ. If the Bible can in any way be said to "contain the whole revelation," this is certainly true of the sacraments as well.

Although Catholic writers do insist on the interrelation of revelation and sacraments, their lack of complete integration of the two often becomes evident in the expressions that they use. When it is said, for example, that Christ left a church structure constituted by apostolic college, revelation, and sacraments, it is clear that revelation is assumed to be something

125

which is possessed by the Church (presumably in books) alongside of other things.[20] When it is said: "The sacrament accomplishes what has been begun by revelation and faith. This is why Christ confided to his Church the double ministry of word and sacrament";[21] the underlying assumption is the identification of word and revelation. Though this terminology could be justified in some contexts it does not seem helpful in explaining the relation of sacrament and revelation. Sacraments do not complete what revelation begins; nothing completes the revelation of earth except the eternal revelation of heaven. There is only the one way to salvation, the way of revelation-faith lived to the end. The sacrament is a peak along this way. Far from being an addition or a parallel to revelation, the sacrament is a bright flash in the mystery of revelation now taking place. As patristic and medieval theologians taught, it is in the sacraments that men are "illuminated" with God's revelation.[22]

What has been said of the liturgy in general is preëminently true of the holy Eucharist. If all of Christian revelation is concentrated symbolically in the liturgy, we are correct in saying that the liturgy is in turn recapitulated in the Eucharist. If the Lord himself is present in the Eucharist, obviously this sacrament can be said to "contain the whole revelation." "The word of revelation infinitely surpasses all that the word that testifies can possibly contain; and this superfluity becomes available to the Church in the living eucharistic presence."[23] It is especially clear in St. John's gospel that the Eucharist is the source of that knowledge which is salvific. By eating the bread of the Eucharist the believer comes into contact with Jesus sent by the Father to give knowledge of salvation (Jn. 6:51; 7:37).

[20] See Eugene Joly, *What is Faith?* (New York, Hawthorn, 1958), p. 123.

[21] Latourelle, *op. cit.*, p. 415.

[22] See *S.T.* III, p. 65, a. 5; F. X. Durrwell, *In the Redeeming Christ* (New York, Sheed and Ward, 1963), pp. 226–228.

[23] Urs von Balthasar, *Word and Revelation*, p. 20.

In the Eucharist men's eyes are opened to the meaning of God's revelation (Lk. 24:31).[24]

The Church celebrates the Eucharist in order to become the Eucharist; the Eucharist is the Church at her best. This sign of unity and bond of charity reveals to the Church what she ought to be and what she is slowly becoming. When the faith of the Church is fully actuated, contact is made with him who embodies the fullness of revelation. In this activity the Church reaches the meeting point of time and eternity where the risen Lord casts the light of understanding on past, present, and future. "The Church is not torn apart by being thus oriented toward the opposite ends of her time, for she is linked to a single fact expressed at both ends of her history on earth, at one end as inauguration, at the other as consummation and every Eucharist is a revelation of it for the time that lies between."[25]

CHRISTIAN LOVE AS REVELATORY

If it is important to keep inwardly related the proclamation of the scriptural word and the symbolic gesture of the sacrament, it is equally important to keep this whole liturgical complex related to the rest of Christian life. Liturgy is meant to be in symbol what the whole of Christian life is to be in fact, that is, a living before God in faith and worship, a believing and responding to the God who reveals. God is revealed as the God of love, and henceforth every morally good act, that is, every act formed by charity, is a revelation of God. Every word of truth and love, every hand extended in kindness, echoes the inner life of the Trinity. "Witness to him is given in every word of love and truth, for every word of truth and love is

[24] Pierre Benoit, *The Eucharist in the New Testament* (Baltimore, Helicon, 1964), p. 86.
[25] Durrwell, *Resurrection*, p. 329.

disturbing to mankind which is tempted by lying and hatred and subject to the power of untruthfulness. . . . Deeds of love make God credible."[26]

Every action which has its roots in the Christian life of the Spirit is an act both revelatory and redeeming; not, of course, by adding to Christ's revelation-redemption, but by sharing his love made full in the Spirit. Every good act of the Christian is capable of being revelatory of God, while at the same time this act draws forth the best that is in other men. The revealing love embodied in gestures and words gives confidence to the loved one to seek the ideal which love holds out. Because love excludes nothing, does not negate anything human or divine, the Christian act of love contains indefinite depths of meaning. Indeed, because an act of charity is the work of the Holy Spirit, the moral activity of the Christian implicitly "contains the whole revelation," provided that nothing is intentionally excluded.

This last statement is nothing more than a reformulation of the traditional teaching that the simple, unlettered Christian attains the whole of orthodox faith by believing and adhering to the Church's teaching. Christian faith can be transmitted by a person who is unaware of all the subtleties of dogma. Very likely, we have not always appreciated what this means in considering the revelatory power of a single good Christian life and even more so of a Christian community. Christ is the revelation of God; the Christian by participation is a revelatory sign not only by preaching or teaching, but by the whole of personal existence.

The true followers of Christ, therefore, are tradition at its most living, the place where God's revelation can shine forth in its sacramentality. "This sacrament is dispensed in daily life, not in Church; in conversation, not during a sermon. It is admin-

[26] Michael Schmaus, *Essence of Christianity* (Chicago, Scepter, 1961), p. 234.

istered not in prayer and meditation, but in situations where prayer shows that it is genuine and where meditation results in the apostolate. There it will be decided whether I have received his Body and Blood in Church effectively."[27]

The Catholic believes that God has really taken hold of humanity, has become incarnate in humanity in such a way that *man* and not merely words can bear God's revelation, can reveal God to others. Never does man become the dominant partner, never does man possess revelation as something distinct from God; but it is nevertheless in man that God's revelation takes place. "God speaks his word within man. Not only what man utters but all that he is becomes God's organ of communication. What man is and can be is only revealed in its fullness when God makes of him his alphabet, his sounding board and sense organ."[28]

The incarnation of the Son of God revealed the possibilities of human nature and showed that the closer man comes to God and the more fully he is transformed by God, the more truly human he is. With equal force the incarnation showed that God's revealing act becomes the more luminous the more deeply it is incarnated in the human. The ideal is not the minimum of human corruption to a divine message, but the maximum of human receptiveness to a divine life. To think that revelation is encased in doctrines taught by the apostles and not changed since that time would be to deny that God gave himself to *man*. Not first in books or institutions, doctrines or rituals, is God's revelation to be met, but in people. Man is for man the way to God. In taking hold of one man, God took hold of all men; in bringing the law and prophecy to summation in a single human life, he made this man the revelation of God. Thus it is that revelation can be shone forth adequately only in people;

[27] Hans Urs von Balthasar, *Science, Religion and Christianity* (Westminster, Newman, 1958), p. 150.
[28] Urs von Balthasar, *Word and Revelation,* p. 108.

129

first, in the person of Jesus Christ, and second, in the person of everyone who lives in Christ.[29]

To say that all the law is summed up in charity (Gal. 5:14) was for Paul equivalent to saying that the law is Christ (Gal. 6:2). It was not a new set of laws which needed revealing, nor did Christ come to reveal some nuances of the old laws. Instead, he both validated and transcended all previous law by revealing the greatness of the person. The way to God was shown to be not through formalized precepts, but through a personal revelation. The way *from* God to man is through Christ and his brothers; the way *to* God is through Christ and his brothers. The Christian moral life, therefore, is judged by God's continuing revelation in people. Only with this conception of God's revelatory action in the world through Christ and his Body the Church, do we have an adequate basis for a moral theology. The fundamental moral law for the Christian is the person of Jesus Christ as reflected in each age in the face of mankind. The Christian is called to live in the moment-to-moment conscious and free acceptance of God's will for him in imitation of Jesus' attitude before his Father. The norm for deciding what God demands of the Christian will not only be universal laws of reason and defined doctrinal truths, but the revelation which denies neither of these but goes beyond both of them. From the power of Christ's continuing humanity, all that is human has become revelational of God. All that is truly human must be accepted and transformed by his love.[30]

[29] See Karl Rahner, "Reflexions théologiques sur l'Incarnation," in *Sciences ecclésiastiques,* XII (1960), p. 15.

[30] Rahner, "Current Problems . . . ," *loc. cit.,* p. 188. The author points out that the study of the theological virtues has almost nothing about Christ in it. This failure springs not from a simple omission or a mistaken formulation, but from a lack of understanding of Christ's reception of God's revelation in an attitude which is archetypal for the Christian's faith, hope, and charity.

VII.

The Church's Understanding
within the Revelational Process

MUCH of what we have said in the previous chapters is not unacceptable to many who do not belong to the Catholic Church. We must now take up the question which seems to divide Protestants and Catholics very sharply in their approach to divine revelation. Catholic teaching has a "doctrinal side," an insistence upon dogmatic formulas, that seems to put it at odds with the thinking of many people today including that of other Christian believers. Indeed, the supposed Catholic reduction of revelation to objects and truths taught by the Church and the corresponding reduction of faith to the acceptance of doctrinal formulas is attacked in the severest terms. "The Bible speaks about faith being the same as being in reality allied to Christ; the misunderstanding replaces the real alliance with Christ as *object* of faith, as a truth to be believed. This confusion, this replacing of personal understanding of faith by the intellectual, is probably the most fatal occurrence within the entire history of the Church."[1]

For a Catholic to reply to this charge by saying that he too thinks that faith is encounter and commitment, is not a sufficient

[1] Emil Brunner, *Truth as Encounter* (2nd ed.; Philadelphia, Westminster, 1964), pp. 164–165.

answer. Either revelation comes to the Christian in the form of truths preserved in formulas, or else revelation is not this but something else. If a Catholic wishes to say the latter, then he must also seriously and deeply consider the meaning of the "revealed truths" that are taught in the Catholic Church.

We have seen in the previous chapters that revelation must be considered in view of God's self-donation to man in the historical existence of a representative people and finally in one man's history. The conscious and free reception of the gift was accomplished in full by this one man and is accomplished by other men through participation. What has been given in principle to all men must be ratified by each through an act that is human. The question of faith cannot be that of accepting some things or formulas outside of oneself, but of accepting God in the gracious bestowal that he makes of himself within the human community. God reveals himself as Someone, and the gift of his personal presence and love is always to someone. But because the one to whom God speaks is man, there is implied a doctrinal aspect to revelation that we must now consider. I take up in this chapter three points of inquiry: 1) the doctrinal aspect of revelation to the apostles; 2) doctrinal development through the reflection of Christian people and especially theologians; 3) the official and authoritative teaching in the Church.

Apostolic Doctrinal Understanding

The entire intercourse of God's dealing with men and the gathering together of these activities in one person was called by St. Paul "the mystery." Little by little the plan had unfolded in human history; then in Jesus Christ the plan was made manifest; he is himself the mystery of God. The personal love of God for man shines forth in the humanity of Jesus, but this revelation of God is not something that man can stand outside of and

132

view with objective neutrality. This is so for two reasons. First, no human person can be understood by a simple objective description. Man's concepts are inadequate to the task and can never of themselves reach the freedom of the person.[2] This is all the more true when the person in question is none other than the God-man. Second, and not unrelated to the first, man cannot grasp the revelation from without because he is within it. He cannot comprehend revelation because he is comprehended by it. Only by letting himself be grasped by God's love does he come to some human grasp of the mystery within which he discovers himself. The mystery is a personal reality which encompasses the questioner in his own questioning, for the mystery is not only the person of Jesus Christ, but the relation which every man has to God through his relation to Christ.

Nothing should be more evident (though we constantly tend to obscure it) than the fact that the word "mystery" as it pertains to revelation does not signify unintelligibility and lack of meaning for the Christian life. On the contrary, the word "mystery" as it is used here has exactly the opposite meaning, that is, it signifies a superluminous intelligibility, an inexhaustible depth of meaning. God revealed in Jesus Christ is incomprehensible not because there is nothing to say of him, but because there is always more to say. "Anyone we cannot love remains a mystery to us, a house closed and impenetrable. Christ is a mystery too, but rather for the infinity of his openness, his unlimited comprehensibility."[3]

Anything which can be exhaustively analyzed, anything which can be placed into human statements, is not a mystery. That is to say, if something is not a mystery after it has been made known, it was never a mystery to begin with. Mystery does not cease to be mystery as it is more and more revealed. The more God's "secret" was revealed to Paul, the more could he appreciate

[2] Cirne-Lima, op. cit., pp. 42–60.
[3] Durrwell, In the Redeeming Christ, p. 222.

the depths of God's wisdom, the incomprehensibility of his judgments, and the unsearchableness of his ways (Rom. 11:33).[4]

The "mystery of God" is found in Jesus Christ whose own grasp of the revealing God was certainly not in the form of doctrines about God. The incomprehensible presence of the Logos to the humanity of Jesus was the unsurpassable revelation of God to man. This revelation was only gradually assimilated by Christ into objective and communicable knowledge as he lived the mystery of God, that is, his own existence in the world with other men. His experience could not be exhausted by human statements. Nevertheless, he could during his lifetime make true statements about God, statements which were neither false nor empty.

The apostles shared in this knowledge by living in personal relationship with Christ. He gave them a participation in his life's knowledge, this not primarily by instructing them in doctrine, but by living with them in friendship. Teaching and instruction were, of course, not excluded. As the good rabbi of his time, Christ formed his disciples both by example and by instruction. The apostles participated in revelation by living with someone; their understanding of revelation bore similarity to the understanding one can have of any person. It is true that Jesus was more "mysterious" than any other person, but the human experience of the apostles in the revelational process was nonetheless that of sharing in a personal relationship. The experience of God in their lives could not possibly have been reduced to a set of formulas, judgments, and Church doctrines.

In the apostolic experience, as in all human experience, there was a jumble of impressions, a shifting of attitudes, a convergence of evidence. What man knows always goes beyond what he can bring to full, objective awareness; in the moment

4 See Hans Urs von Balthasar, "The Freedom of the Subject," in *Cross Currents*, XII (Winter, 1962), p. 29.

134

of truth he always knows more than he can express. Man cannot avoid representing his knowledge in concepts and words, but the least reflection makes him realize that his concepts are rooted in a more primordial consciousness not completely expressible. But it is senseless to berate conceptual expressions because they are not exhaustive of human knowledge. Words, ideas, and propositions are indeed limited and defective instruments, but they are so because they are human and are the means by which men communicate their experience and bring to full awareness their own experience.

The global experience of the apostles took place at these several levels of pre-conceptual knowledge and its refraction and reflexive objectification in conceptual judgments. In the case of the apostles there was the additional factor of the Spirit's post-resurrectional assistance in their reflection. This special guidance of the Holy Spirit continued throughout the time of the Church's foundation. The conceptual expression of the apostles' experience became progressively more accurate, or perhaps we should say that their concepts, formulas, and teaching became progressively "less inaccurate." This is not to say that their first statements were false. All their words which were spoken from within the mystery were true to the extent that they gave some insight into the reality that went beyond them. Of any experience there can be many true statements which vary in their capacity to convey the truth to another. It is a false assumption to presume that the more primitive a statement is and the closer in time to the original experience it is, the truer and more accurate it is. By striving to translate their global experience into a communicable form, the apostles heightened their understanding of their own experience.[5]

We know today that the composition of the New Testament followed a long process of human reflection upon the revelation of God in Christ. Holy Scripture is not a divine word fallen from

[5] Rahner, "Development of Dogma," *loc. cit.,* pp. 65–67.

135

heaven or a collection of truths dictated by a divine master. On every page it is manifest that if the Scripture is God's word it is just as truly man's word. "A faith anchored in the Church took over the words of Jesus, disclosed their deeper meaning, cleared up any doubts that arose, and formed the confession of faith."[6]

There is no pure word of God contaminated to varying degrees by human distortion. Instead, the human reception, understanding, and interpretation are intrinsic to the revelation itself. The apostles never ceased to reflect upon what had been given to them. Their thought underwent a development to the point where it could be set in relatively stable formulations for preaching, teaching, and liturgical recital.[7] No sharp break is discernible, no entrance of "Hellenizing tendencies," that added human words to a pure, divine communication. In the dialogue of Israel and Yahweh, of Jesus and his Father, of the apostles and the Trinity, there was always the real humanity of the receiving partner; this human understanding meant a conceptual and verbal expression of God revealing. At each stage in the continuing dialogue there was to some degree human reflection and interpretation and therefore doctrinal formulation and development.[8]

Doctrinal development, then, is not a process which began after the composition of holy Scripture. The Scripture is already a doctrinal formulation, a collection of theological reflections which point to a more primitive experience. This is true of St. Mark's gospel as well as St. John's. The inspired words of holy Scripture are in no way to be undervalued, but it is those very words which point to a reality beyond the words. All later doctrinal development must root itself in holy Scripture, but

[6] Rudolf Schnackenburg, "The Dogmatic Evolution of the New Testament," in Dogmatic vs. Biblical Theology, p. 152.

[7] See Karl Rahner, "Was ist eine dogmatische Aussage?" Schriften zur Theologie, Band V (Einsiedeln, Benziger, 1962), p. 76.

[8] See Otto Semmelroth, "God's Word and Man's Reply," in The Preaching Word (New York, Herder and Herder, 1965), pp. 55–71.

not Scripture understood as a series of "revealed truths." Scripture is not a collection of revealed words and judgments from which deductions can be made. It is rather a testimony of faith to the revelation made full in the conscious experience of Christ and his apostles.

Holy Scripture, therefore, represents to a large degree the theology of the apostles, taking the word "theology" in its widest sense.[9] To some Christians this has seemed scandalous and they have sought for the pure gospel behind the theologizing. Stripping away doctrinal accretions would be a necessary undertaking only if revelation consisted in a series of divine pronouncements. If, on the other hand, revelation is the communion of the God-man and the cognitive aspect of man's life in Christ, neither the most primitive recording of events and words in Jesus' life, nor the formulas of holy Scripture, nor later Church teachings, are in themselves the revelation of God. I insist, however, that to say that neither Scripture nor later Church teaching is the revelation does not deny to either of these a significant role within the revelational process.

DEVELOPMENT IN THE CHURCH

The human reflection upon God's gracious self-giving did not cease with the apostolic Church. Insofar as revelation continued to happen in the Church, Christians continued to experience and to reflect upon revelation. This happened particularly in the community's participation in the liturgy and in the individual's life of Christian charity. At all times the church's reflection was mediated by the privileged testimony of the apostles. Since faith of itself gives birth to further probing and reaching out, the process of reflection and development was shared in by every mature Christian. "An adult is one who, taking cognizance of

[9] See Rahner, "Development of Dogma," *loc. cit.,* p. 66.

what he possesses, reflects thereon, analyzes it, builds up its resources, unifies it. The theologian is an adult Christian who, taking cognizance of what he possesses, reflects upon it, analyzes the complex content of his faith, builds it up, unifies it."[10]

As the ordinary believer does not leave behind the apostolic message or go out from Christ, so also theology in its development never leaves aside Christ or the Scriptures. The study of sacred Scripture is the soul of sacred theology.[11] Theology attempts to understand faith with faith, revelation from within revelation. It hardly needs to be said that theology can fail and often has failed to carry out its chief mission of clarifying revelation, that is, of understanding revelation in the intelligible unity that is founded on the unity of Christ. Theology does have to formulate truths which are not part of revelation; but the function of the whole of theology, nevertheless, is to deepen the understanding of revelation itself.

There is, therefore, a double movement in theology. First, there is a centrifugal movement toward the sciences, toward all that is human, toward the whole of world history, to see all things in the light of the revelatory experience. Second, there is also an inward movement with newly forged conceptual tools and additional information for the enrichment and unification of revelation. When this complete cycle is not operative, theology tends to become the science of drawing logical conclusions with the means thus mistaken for the end. The whole of theology and the whole of Christian life with all of their necessary centrifugal tendencies must gravitate toward the center, toward bringing all into an organic and intelligible unity founded on the fullness of revelation in Christ.

Systematic theology can thus help in the movement from a

---

[10] M. D. Chenu, *Is Theology a Science?* (New York, Hawthorn, 1959), p. 18.
[11] See *Constitution on Divine Revelation,* Chapter VI, Article 24.

living possession of truth on the part of the faithful to a more explicit formulation. The purpose of theology is not to stir up religious feelings, but neither is theology simply a neutral collection of truths. Theology can bring before the Christian mind some particular aspect of revelation that needs special emphasis, and it can work out the logical structures in the movement of understanding and the process of development. There is an indispensable need for work of this kind within the Church. Ultimately, however, it is the Spirit who guides the Christian understanding and who is the principle of continuity in all doctrinal development. The Spirit blows where he wills (Jn. 3:8), a fact that is sometimes dismaying for theologians who look in vain for a logical or deductive link in the process of development. For this reason, no all-inclusive law of doctrinal development can be laid down *a priori;* the perfected law of development can be seen only at the term of the whole process.[12]

The Church, that is, the people communally and hierarchically united to Christ, bears the revelation and is borne by the revelation. The people of the Church always live in relation to a particular world culture which is not simply an element external to revelation. The people must speak of God's revelation from within that world in which they live. By the interaction of man and his world, new concepts and words are formed which may help to express the revelation present from the beginning but not completely brought to explicit consciousness. In the consciousness of Christ there was in some way implicit his own history and all future history. But just as the human experience of Christ was necessary for the development of revelation in his earthly existence, so too, the experience of all peoples and all times is necessary for the complete and perfected revelation in the Church.

[12] See Rahner, "Development of Dogma," *loc. cit.,* p. 44.

AUTHORITATIVE TEACHING

The Church as a whole is the recipient of God's revelation, and each individual participates in revelation according to his position within the community. Despite some appearances to the contrary, the function of the hierarchy in the Church is not to possess and hand down the revelation, but to listen to, to guide, and to protect the faith of the whole Church in the living of revelation. The whole Church has from the beginning a human understanding of God's self-revelation. There is no need for the introduction of an external authority to provide understanding or add to the apostolic testimony. Within the believing Church and within the mystery of revelation, God's guidance has been promised to the entire people of God.

The Church's continuity and its preservation from failure in the divine mission is ultimately the work of the Holy Spirit. However, if the Church is to be truly human, the divine guidance must find human expression in an authority structure. This authority is not opposed to the Spirit, the apostles, or the Scriptures; it is the extension of these set up for the service of the whole Church. "The question outstanding between Protestantism and Catholicism is by no means whether the authority of the Word of God in Scripture can or cannot be limited by some other authority. It is one of determining in what actual conditions, established by God himself as the author of Scripture, their sovereign authority can effectively be upheld in practice."[13]

The role of the magisterium is not to decide the truth or falsity of what is in Scripture, but to ascertain the truth or falsity of individual interpretations that appear in the course of time. Far from eliminating all "private interpretation," the existence of a magisterium ought to be the guarantee that every sector of the Church and every individual within the Church can contribute an understanding of revelation. In this way it is the

[13] Bouyer, *Word, Church and Sacrament*, p. 28.

140

Church which provides the interpretive norm and not someone's school of theology.

The teaching authority in the Church looks not only to her scholars investigating ancient documents; it also looks within to her living consciousness and to the revelatory activity in which the people of God is now immersed.[14] The continuing presence of a teaching authority in the Church is the sign of the continuing actuality of revelation. A revelation that could be placed in a book or a creed would be that of a God of the dead who had retired from his world leaving his truths behind him. But the revelation between living people emerges today in the hearing, understanding, and interpretation of the teaching Church. The teaching authority of the present-day Church in interpreting the Scriptures extends into our world the same apostolic teaching authority that wrote the Scriptures.[15]

Provided we do not separate the teaching office in the Church from the believing Church, and provided we do not separate the whole Church from Christ, then the doctrinal statements of the Church will appear neither as distortions nor as rationalizations.[16] I have said that the knowing in revelation takes place in man at a deeper level than that of the conceptual and verbal; but I have also stressed that this is no reason to deprecate the formulation of knowledge in concepts and words. Without an interior word knowledge is not human; without an exterior word knowledge is not social. If a human understanding of God's revelation is to form a Christian community, it must have its "sacramental expression" in human terms. The knowledge which is at stake here and its correct formulation is not something lightly to be considered. The question as Rahner has

---

[14] See Walter J. Burghardt, "Catholic Concept of Tradition in the Light of Modern Theological Thought," in *Proceedings: Catholic Theological Society of America*, 6 (1951), p. 67; Dhanis, *loc. cit.*, pp. 233–234.

[15] See *Constitution on Divine Revelation*, Chapter II, Article 7.

[16] See Mersch, *op. cit.*, pp. 409–410.

141

formulated it, is "whether we have in fact by knowledge laid hold of the absolute reality itself, because in such a grasp, which is essentially, though not exclusively, an act of cognition, salvation itself consists."[17]

The formula, of course, is not the reality. The Church has never claimed that her formulas are "passwords" rather than signs. The doctrinal teaching of the Church is the outer, corporeal aspect of a reality that transcends all words and yet must be symbolized verbally if it is thoroughly to penetrate human existence. Such formulas necessarily move away from the dialogic structures which characterize revelation, but not in order to create a system of truths that the Church would then teach as the revelation. The assent of Christian faith is not to the truths which the Church teaches, but to God who speaks in Jesus Christ and in the continuing revelatory sign which is his Church. The Church does not stand between God and man obstructing man's direct communication with God, nor is the Church part of the formal motive of faith.[18] The Church and the teaching authority within the Church must be obedient to the Word made flesh and to the word of Scripture. There is a teaching authority to see that the Word and his word can be intelligibly heard by *everyone* in the Church.

The Church professes her belief in God by the prayer of her creeds. The several creeds drawn up in the early Church are not so much teachings of doctrine as brief confessions of faith. To forget that the creed is a prayer is to miss the point of bringing together the doctrinal statements only in order to bring together the Christian community in the unity of its prayer of faith. The creed, to be sure, can function as a norm for the individual Christian who can thereby judge whether he belongs to the Church universal, but it is never a norm to replace the

[17] Karl Rahner, *On Heresy* (New York, Herder and Herder, 1964), p. 14.
[18] See Aubert, *op. cit.*, pp. 689–702.

Church's objective norm of holy Scripture. If the Roman Catechism had meant that revelation can be reduced to creed, sacraments, commandments, and the Lord's Prayer so that there would remain nothing else to say of revelation, then it would be open to the severest criticism. On the other hand, it is quite a different matter to provide for Christian people an intelligible and prayerful summary of Christian revelation which goes beyond all words.[19]

It is a regrettable but undeniable fact that indolent teachers and pastors have thought that they had automatically transmitted revelation because they had taught Christian doctrine and had had the creed memorized. But this is the fault neither of creed nor of doctrinal formulas, but of human beings. It is due to the failure of men who do not understand that doctrine derives its meaning from Christian life and finds its purpose only in return to that life, that formulas separated from the revelatory action of God in man's social life can constitute a positive hindrance to revelation, that what is always at issue in Christianity is God in his communication with man and man in his temporal, bodily, communal existence with God and his fellow men.

In defining doctrines, therefore, the Church's intention is not to disintegrate the "mystery" of God's self-gift to the world and his invitation to man to take part in the divine life. The Church throughout her whole history has had to wage a battle against the ever present human temptation to destroy mystery and to reduce revelation to facile answers which would put man in control instead of God. Because revelation is something that goes beyond man, something that lifts man out of his complacency, and something that reveals the sinfulness of man, he revolts against revelation and tries to bring it down to the purely

[19] See *Catechism of the Council of Trent* (New York, Joseph F. Wagner, 1923), p. 9: "Our predecessors in the faith have very wisely reduced all the doctrines of salvation to these four heads: The Apostles' Creed, the Sacraments, the Ten Commandments, and the Lord's Prayer."

conceptual level where there are no mysteries, but only subjects and objects.[20] Almost all heresies have had this trait in common: the reduction of the mystery of revelation to the system of human logic. Against these heretical formalizations the Church directs her dogmatic definitions not in order to give the "correct explanation" of the mystery, but to protect the mystery from the prying rationalism of men.[21]

When the mystery of God's revelation is lived in the simplicity of direct awareness and is reflected upon by those who live within the mystery, the Church in her official teaching has little reason to interfere. When, however, conflict from within or opposition from without brings the Church's reflective consciousness fully into operation, it becomes necessary for official teachers to act so as to protect the living faith of all. The doctrinal judgments are not intended to destroy the life but to make its continuance possible. "We often hear it said: Dogmas are mere rationalizations, pure conceptualizations of that which ought to remain living. He who says this shows that he has not understood what they are about. Of course, dogmas contain ideas and abstract thoughts; but if we look more closely to see how these thoughts are put together and how the different ideas are related to one another, we see that they are placed around the mystery in order to protect it. The dogma is a solid fortress or protective ring surrounding the source, the depth, the life."[22]

So long as man lives humbly and reverently within the revelation of God, there are no limits to his receptive possibilities for truth and freedom. Since God, the Infinite and Absolute, is being revealed in Christ and his members, all of the truth attained by an individual or by the Church simply opens out

[20] Romano Guardini, *The Life of Faith* (Westminster, Newman, 1961), pp. 116–117.

[21] See Michael Schmaus, *Katholische Domatik*, Band I (München, Hueber, 1960), p. 81; Urs von Balthasar, *Word and Redemption*, p. 15.

[22] Guardini, *Life of Faith*, p. 118.

upon the greater inexhaustible depths of God's love.[23] The progress of doctrinal development is not the gradual exhaustion of a certain amount of material or a number of truths to be found. "Upon those who are truly poor, who truly thirst after it, the Spirit pours out the consolation of his truth in such breathtaking, ever increasing abundance that the very notion of 'using it up,' if it ever occurred to them, could only strike them as ludicrous blasphemy."[24]

Even conciliar definitions are more in the nature of starting points or frameworks within which to live and work than of conclusions. Each of the truths reached in the Church's progress is intended to bring into greater unity the witness to a revelation which is refracted through but never bottled up in human statements. The truth which the Church has taken possession of she does not then leave behind; but every ecclesial formulation, while itself remaining valid, can in principle be improved upon through reformulation. Language itself is continually changing, and if revelation is to be intelligible for all men, then the language of living men must constantly be taken into account, and used as much as possible in the Church's formulations. The Church can to a limited extent create her own vocabulary and attach to words definite and unchangeable meanings; but even so, as we have indicated, it would be some anomaly were the Church, determined now more than ever to be a living force in human life, to speak to men in an antiquated, if however precise, language. This does not mean that the Church must simply substitute new words for old ones, but must also reintegrate past ways of speaking into better modes of communication.[25]

We should also note that doctrinal pronouncements that the Church makes from time to time within the context of defend-

---

[23] See Jean Daniélou, "Unité et pluralité de la pensée chrétienne," in *Etudes*, CCCXII (January, 1962), p. 11.

[24] Urs von Balthasar, *Theology of History*, p. 103.

[25] See Rahner, "Was ist . . . ," *loc. cit.*, pp. 69–70.

ing one or various of the truths she is committed to teach and uphold, tend to bring particular aspects of her life and message very much to the forefront. More than is ordinarily true of human judgment, a polemical or defensive statement, even when true, must be seen in context, and requires the counter-balance of other truths.[26] Although some people may bewail the possibility of a failure in perspective or may try to pre-tend that the Church possesses a system of truths untouched by the scars of human frailty, the nature of the Church's mission demands that she live in an inescapable dialectical tension with the ever shifting world-view in which she finds herself. Through the presence of the Holy Spirit the ultimate success of her mission is guaranteed, but there is no guarantee that she will always say the best thing, in the best way, at the best possible time. Neither does the Spirit's guidance provide that a single doctrine or word can be torn from her life and brandished as a "revealed truth" from God. She does speak the truth from within revelation, but each of these truths has its full and properly balanced meaning only within the entire organism of Christ and his Church.

[26] See Küng, *Structures of the Church,* p. 393.

VIII.

Individual Participation in Revelation

THROUGHOUT our previous chapters we have stressed the communal or social character of revelation. There were two main reasons for doing this. First, the Bible always focuses upon the community of God's people as the recipient of God's revelatory-redemptive activity. Second, it is impossible to appreciate any human activity without recognizing its social dimension. The nature of man as a social being has been at times obscured or even denied. However, for a multiplicity of reasons, of which sheer numbers is not the least, the question of community has now become central to modern thought. Furthermore, the irreversibility of modern social changes (for example, in technology, transportation, communications media) makes it certain that the human community will become an ever more dominant concern. Thus, our attempt to relate revelation to the person within community is based upon no passing fad even though the communal emphasis in Catholic theology may appear somewhat novel.

In this chapter I would like to make a few additional precisions about the individual person in revelatory activity. Far from leaving the community to deal with the individual, throughout this consideration I presuppose that the individual becomes a person only in and through community. A naïve, "common-sense" philosophy always tends to oppose these two, person and

147

community; in addition, daily experience does involve actual conflicts that are not fully resolvable. Nevertheless, men have become increasingly aware that proposals to escape from the social question are of little use. As a number of modern thinkers have expressed it, man's eventual choice of a style of living is reduced to two alternatives: either to construct a mechanized, depersonalized organization which will differ but little from an ant heap, or else to form a personal and organic society based upon principles of love.[1]

God's revelation, as we have seen, emerges from a community that already exists. More important still, revelation is directed to the perfection of the community of God's interlocutors eventually to be the whole of mankind. To form this community of his people God takes hold of individual persons where the centers of freedom are. It is this individual revelational experience with which we are here concerned. We look first to the emergence of revelation in the person and second to the relation between this revelation and freedom.

INDIVIDUAL EMERGENCE

The individual lives today in a world which has been taken hold of by God's Spirit. God has become incarnate in a human nature, changing forever the relation of humanity to God. Every man is born into a supernatural order and is oriented toward a supernatural end before he becomes consciously and reflexively aware of it. Furthermore, Catholic belief maintains that baptism, even baptism of infants, works a real ontological change, a new creation, by which man is taken into the Body of Christ.

The triune God gives himself personally to the knowledge

[1] See Gabriel Marcel, *Men Against Humanity* (London, Harvill Press, 1952), p. 140; Pierre Teilhard de Chardin, *The Future of Man* (New York, Harper and Row, 1964), p. 54.

and love of man even before man can consciously share the experience. To some Protestants this doctrine has seemed unintelligible, but what we are here positing is simply the extension of the relation Christ's redemption has to all men. It is true that God does not overwhelm human freedom and that in one sense he waits upon man's free choice. Nevertheless, this does not prevent God from bestowing his gifts upon man before man can consciously ask for them. God creates man and endows him with numerous gifts culminating in God's own personal presence. This self-donation of God to the individual is the basis for the revelation-redemption which transforms the individual Christian and anyone who is seeking the God of Jesus Christ though it be only implicitly.

Restricting ourselves in this chapter to the Christian situation, we may say that God gives himself to man in an act of grace and from this self-communication there issues the conscious revelatory experience. Man does not first know God by faith and revelation and then, having been united by knowledge, proceed to another kind of union.[2] Rather, God takes hold of man by his indwelling Spirit and this results in the ontological reaction we call sanctifying grace and the beginning of a conscious presence to self of God's activity which we call revelation. In the person of Christ, the immediate intuition of God which issues in revelation stems from the ontological bond of union with the Logos. In an analagous way, for those who live in Christ their knowledge is also given with their mode of being. The Christian's share in God's revelation "is the actuation, in the order of knowledge, of what this manner of existence is in the order of being. Therefore, it is the expression, under the form of knowledge, of that which, in the reality of things, is the gift of God to men in Christ."[3] The foundation of the individual's

---

[2] See Karl Rahner, "Some Implications of the Scholastic Concept of Uncreated Grace," *Theological Investigations,* vol. I, p. 328.

[3] Mersch, *op. cit.,* p. 88.

revelatory experience, therefore, resides in the gracious presence of the Spirit who penetrates human existence at its highest point, thus affecting "the *a priori* 'mental horizon' which we are conscious of in being conscious of ourselves."[4]

To be a spiritual being is to be a conscious being; to be a supernatural being is to be a supernaturally conscious being with a consciousness that wells up out of life culminating and directing that life. The emergence of a supernatural knowledge from supernatural life differs, of course, from the immanentism taught by modernists. God is not to be confused with man. It is the infinitely transcendent God who by the power of his Spirit freely makes possible man's supernatural knowledge.[5] God works with man's person in an organic way since it is man in his entirety and integrity that God desires. He does not intermittently offer "truths" for man's mind. Instead, he begins by knowing and loving man with a love that is transforming. When that divine activity in man's life emerges into conscious experience, man comes to know the one who is closer to him than he is to himself.

Through the life communicated to man, God is continuously whispering in the human heart. There is a dynamism to all life but especially to this life which pushes it forward toward conscious realization. However, as Aubert points out, "the voice of God is most often a murmur which requires sustained attention in order to be heard."[6] This attention is often more than man is capable of maintaining, so that although a life has been given to him he is yet incapable of grasping its meaning. If God were to give no further help to man's understanding, revelation might remain on an inchoate and unexplicated level. Therefore, God completes the revelational process by speaking words of human love. Like a mother speaking to a child God

[4] Rahner, *Nature and Grace*, p. 129.

[5] See Jean Mouroux, *The Christian Experience* (New York, Sheed and Ward, 1954), p. 72.

[6] Aubert, *op. cit.*, p. 775.

draws forth from the pre-reflexive, entitative, and intentional union a wealth of meaning. "They have treasures in their souls which they will never be able to express, but which they ought to express since they are spiritual beings. Then God, using human words, the only words his little ones understand, describes to them the marvelous beings they have become. What he tells them is what their very nature as members strives to tell them, so much is it their own, but does not succeed, so amazing is the beauty."[7]

The revelatory experience for the individual is thus made complete by the word drawing grace into the conscious experience of faith.[8] This is the Church's intention in her mission of preaching, teaching, and interpreting holy Scripture. God's inspired words bring to conscious and reflexive awareness the meaning of revelation. In this way holy Scripture as it exists within the Church becomes the interpretive norm for man's religious experience.

The written and preached word, however, is intended to be incarnated in human beings. The word will have its most powerful effect only when it appears in another person who embodies the gospel in his life. Much has been written in recent years on the notion of "witness" and the transmission of Christian revelation through the witness of Christian life. This centrality of witness is not a passing fad, nor is it founded merely on a belief that "actions speak louder than words." What is in question here and what is in need of further analysis in theological literature, is the nature of knowledge and the nature of Christian revelation itself.

Man is born into the world with an unlimited capacity to know but utterly lacking the knowledge and the animal instincts necessary for taking care of himself. Man's dependency

[7] Mersch, op. cit., p. 83; see Constitution on Divine Revelation, Chapter III, Article 13.

[8] See the summary of Mouroux, Christian Experience, pp. 55–60, on the teaching of Aquinas and Augustine concerning the experience of faith.

upon others is both more pronounced and more extended than other animals. Though infinitely rich in possibilities, man is incapable of revealing himself to himself. But because the world into which he is born is a humanized world bearing the imprint of generations in its culture, art, science, and language,[9] and because the lives of all men are inextricably interwoven and the world of nature itself is bound with man in his destiny, everything speaks to man of man, unveiling to him his possibilities and transmitting to him all that men of the past have laboriously discovered. To know what a person is, man must meet a person, that is, a free man who can give himself or refuse himself through love.

In experiencing a person, in having a word spoken not in general but to him alone, man recognizes his own being as a person and the actuality of love and freedom. Without language man cannot become conscious of what he is; without a word spoken to him in respect and love, he cannot become conscious of who he is. Only through the loving word of another can man discover his own uniqueness and the destiny of his created freedom. To the degree that man is opened by another to communion with man and God, his relation to that other is true and personalizing; thererby is deepened the realization of what he is and what he can become. In the fellowship of man, man discovers what it means to be man; there he finds the power to move forward the realization of the human project.

It should not be surprising, therefore, that God reveals to the individual Christian what it means to be a Christian in the face of another Christian. If it were the mind, the soul, or some abstract human nature that were at issue, then it would be conceivable that revelation could be by an interior movement or a written doctrine. However, since it is *man,* the being of bodily, temporal, social existence, who is to be Christian, revela-

---

[9] See Albert Dondeyne, *Faith and the World* (Pittsburgh, Duquesne University, 1963), pp. 179–190; Peter Schoonenberg, *God's World in the Making* (Pittsburgh, Duquesne University, 1964), pp. 1–35.

tion must take place in a human life and in a communion of human individuals. Man discovers what it means to be a Christian first in the person of Jesus Christ, and second in the person of those who are following Christ in Christian love.[10] We are not here on the level of metaphor or moral applications, but on the ontological bedrock of Christian revelation. In the gesture of love on the part of a Christian, God's revelation happens.

The human, historical condition that I have previously spoken of means on the level of the individual believer the same as it did in the history of Israel, namely, a slow and painful progress toward the understanding of revelation and the growth of freedom. There is a rhythm in this historical and bodily life that must be respected; this means that there is no way, human or divine, whereby suddenly everything can be revealed to another. Every bodily gesture of true love reveals something of divine love, yet the bodily also veils what is deepest in man. The bodily nature of man is always inhibitive of a total self-giving. Concupiscence, moreover, as the effect of an original fall, tends to increase this drag of nature.[11]

There is a temptation even for the most ardent advocate of God's revelation to try to escape from the rhythm inherent to this bodily life. But what is true of dialogue between men is also true of divine revelation: there must be both silence and speaking; there must be periods in which nothing is apparently happening, while below consciousness a replenishment is taking place; there must be a respect for what the individual is actually capable of giving at each concrete moment of his life.[12] There is no less exacting way than this of creating the truth; there is no other way to help establish man in God's love than by respecting

[10] See Alfonso Nebreda, "Role of Witness in Transmitting the Message," in *Pastoral Catechetics,* edited by Johannes Hofinger and Theodore C. Stone (New York, Herder and Herder, 1964), pp. 67–86.
[11] See Rahner's essay on the nature of concupiscence, in *Theological Investigations,* vol. I, pp. 347–382.
[12] See Josef Goldbrunner, *Holiness is Wholeness* (New York, Pantheon, 1955), p. 33.

the historical character of human existence. Since revelation is the act of a participating subject becoming aware of his communion with God and man, it should be obvious that such things as violence, social pressure, or mass advertising techniques cannot be the means of communicating revelation.[13] Only the man who is patient and who is willing to let God and the human individual work out the revelation for themselves can be an instrument of God in that revelation.

REVELATION AND FREEDOM

Implicit in this discussion has been a certain conception of the relation between knowledge and love, truth and freedom. This is a point which needs some further comment. I said earlier that a dichotomy of mind and body works devastating consequences upon a theology of revelation. To overcome this split it is insufficient simply to insist that the body *also* plays a part. A more radical kind of thinking and a different style of living are needed to rediscover the unity of man that precedes any distinction between body and soul. If man is divided at the start, then all attempts to restore unity by bringing the parts together prove fruitless. We are not, of course, denying that there is basis for a distinction or distinctions within the unity of man; but on the other hand, that the common presentation of such distinctions in catechism and theology manuals is at variance with revelation is hardly deniable either.[14] This is not a simple error of fact which can be corrected by changing a few words and doctrines.

[13] See Dondeyne, *Faith and the World,* p. 61.

[14] See Paul Chauchard, *Science and Religion* (New York, Hawthorn, 1962), p. 23: "By separating the soul from the body, Descartes opened the door to materialism. It is a curious fact, but this idea so opposed both to Thomist philosophy and to biblical metaphysics, seems to have been implicitly granted by many theologians, because it allowed them to keep apart the two fields, that of the body, reserved to science, and that of the soul, belonging wholly to religion."

The failure to read the inspired word of God, the failure to reflect deeply upon human existence, the failure to live with a clear consciousness of and courage in being a Christian, the failure to participate bodily and socially in worship—all these must lead to an escape from history, community, and matter to an unreal world where God's word is a formula, where God's law is a code, and where the worship of God consists in the protection of one's soul from nature, other people, and one's own body.

Part of the manifestation of the failure to understand *man* as the one who stands before God in Christ through the revelatory love of the Spirit, is the separation of man's intellect from his will. Catholic theologians are striving to see the inner unity of the intellectual and volitional in the act of faith, but there is need for more examination of the question at the deepest levels, biblically, philosophically, theologically, pastorally.[15] If this is not done, there is danger of rephrasing statements of fact without a basic reorientation of attitudes. We have long had many of the right phrases quoted from St. Thomas, but this did not save us from an external juxtaposition of intellect and will in the actual presentations of faith and revelation.

Man's relation to God, both in the order of creation and in the gift of his grace in Son and Spirit, is a dynamism which precedes the conceptual activity of man's reasoning power and the choice of his will. Man's openness to being is the ontological ground out of which both reflexive knowledge and free choice proceed and back to which they lead to set man more solidly in being, the place where truth and goodness are one.[16] The

[15] See Robert Johann, "Experience and Philosophy," in *Experience, Existence and the Good,* edited by Irwin C. Lieb (Carbondale, Ill., Southern Illinois University, 1961), pp. 25–38; Joseph de Finance, "Being and Subjectivity," in *Cross Currents,* VI (Spring, 1956), pp. 163–178.

[16] See Frederick Crowe, "Complacency and Concern in the Thought of St. Thomas," in *Theological Studies,* XIX (June, 1959), pp. 206–210; Urs von Balthasar, "The Freedom . . . ," *loc. cit.,* pp. 15–16.

fundamental stance of man's being toward being as such does not exist as an isolated act in itself, but exists as refracted through the intellectual and volitional. Every human act is an act of knowing and loving; there are not two acts that are closely related, but a single, concrete act within which knowledge and love can be distinguished.

The reciprocity and inner union of knowledge and love reflect not only the primordial ground of man's unity, but the concrete history of his personal unity as well. How a particular man acts in a concrete instance is largely determined by the history of his individual life. Day by day man solidifies a position *vis-à-vis* the whole of being. It is a grave fallacy to assume that man can do anything he wants with himself if only he "wills" it strongly enough. Man's real choices lie in the gradual building up of a unified position and in the slow erosion of a past position. In all cases he must accept his past history and live in accord with it. Every attempt to escape his own past or to do violence with it can only be illusory or self-destructive.[17]

Man's act of knowing-loving is not only a symbolization of his past history unified within the present, it is also an embodiment of his hopes and future destiny. What is true of the past is also true of the future; that is, there is an ultimate point of unity where goodness and truth are self-encompassing, but there is also an immediate fragmentation at a point where the good that man seeks and the truth that he knows seem to separate. The objects of intellect and will can in fact be distinguished, but knowledge and love are still related by an inner reciprocal causality. Though it is true that man's loves are determined by what he knows, it is equally true that his knowledge is determined by his loves. How he stands toward the whole of being is measured at every instant by his past history and by his life projected toward the future.

This analysis of the unity of past and future in man's present could be extended to great length. Enough has been said, how-

[17] Goldbrunner, *Holiness is Wholeness*, p. 36.

ever, to establish a basis for seeing the inner relation of knowledge and love in man's openness to 1) objects 2) persons 3) God.

Even in relation to the world of the non-personal, man cannot bracket his past existence. He finds himself in a situation with attitudes that have been in development since before he was consciously aware of them. He never approaches the world neutrally, nor can he look with disinterested gaze upon an area of simple, straightforward "facts" that are unconnected with his attitudes or freedom. There is a kind of revelation in which being presents itself and speaks to man. There is correspondingly a kind of listening and consent to being, an awareness of nature in order to understand it. The philosopher does not simply look at the world, rather he sits before it in wonder.[18]

The attempts to imitate in every sphere the methods of empirical science and mathematics can lead to the apotheosis of pure objectivity and the consequent abstraction of intellectual activity from the rest of human life. Scientists themselves in this century have come to question to what extent a spectator approach is possible or desirable within empirical science. Whatever judgment they may make on their own field of learning, it is certain that in most areas outside of empirical science, a true objectivity is not reached by the spectator. The truth is attained not by holding back from involvement with the object and by a lack of concern, but by a subjective openness and a readiness to accept, interpret, and approve. There can be no question of eliminating love or "will" even in the most speculative question, but of having the right attitudes and the love proper to the occasion.[19] As a man loves more truly, in a way proper to the object, his knowledge becomes more profound. Conversely, a failure in moral attitude, a selfishness and hatred, cloud his understanding and turn him from the truth.

What is true of man's relation to objects of nature is much

[18] See Joseph Pieper, *Leisure, the Basis of Culture* (New York, Pantheon, 1952), pp. 89–146.
[19] See Crowe, *loc. cit.*, p. 213; Maréchal, *op. cit.*, p. 406.

157

more strikingly true of his relation to other people. At this level the ever present dialectic of knowledge and love which can be obscured in non-personal knowledge becomes evident. I have said that even on the non-personal level there is a kind of revelation, that is, a speaking of the world and a receptiveness and response by man. When there is question of two persons knowing each other then there is revelation in the proper sense: a mutual exchange of giving and receiving that establishes a communion in knowing. Of course, another person can be described in the same way as things of nature, but what constitutes the person as a unique, free individual can be attained only by his revealing himself. There must be a free bestowal and a free acceptance or else there is no knowledge that is truly personal. The act of acceptance is itself a kind of bestowal, the primary gift that engenders trust between persons. Once this relationship in trust and love is established there is a natural dynamism which supports a continuing revelation. There are no inherent limits to the development and deepening of this revelation, since human beings never reach through all appearances to the ultimate truth of the person, and since human life is always, as it were, ahead of itself.

Since personal being and freedom are always attained by this natural, human revelation, personal knowledge always contains a faith element. To know a person in the uniqueness of his existence, one must believe in him and the revelation he makes of himself. The free certitude of faith ("moral certitude") that can be reached here is not a lesser kind of certitude in an area in which better methods of study are not yet available. The fundamental option for being and truth, manifesting itself in the free receptivity of faith toward other persons, is the gateway to the fullness of truth. Without faith and freedom man is cut off from the highest level of truth.[20]

[20] See Guardini, *Life of Faith,* p. 59; Max Scheler, *The Nature of Sympathy* (London, Routledge and Kegan Paul, 1954), pp. 147–161.

While remaining, therefore, on a natural and philosophical level, we may say that faith and revelation can no longer be considered peripheral questions applying only where a second-hand knowledge is available. On the contrary, faith and revelation are the conditions for the appearance of being in the fullness of its intelligibility. The faith that grounds man in the truth is a fundamental passivity which is the very opposite of non-activity. This intensely human act of complete receptivity is the universal *a priori* by which man accepts all as having more meaning than he himself is capable of seeing and judging.[21]

Personal knowledge is a rising toward unity and at the same time a regrounding of knowledge and love in the unity from which they originally sprang. This convergence at both ends gives hint to a final unity which man does not reach in natural revelation. Christianity is the announcement that there is an ultimate depth (or height) of human existence where knowing and decision, truth and goodness, are no longer separable. At that point of existence man is related to the God who is the presupposition of human freedom and intentionality and at the same time their fulfillment.

Philosophy and religion, as they approach this point where all merges into unity, must struggle against an all-enveloping absolutism which threatens to overwhelm man's individual existence. By a strange kind of paradox, Christianity goes to what looks like the brink of pantheism, looks clearly into the abyss, and thereby avoids the fall. Going to the ultimate in uniting the divine and human within a single person who lived, died, and rose, Christianity is the one religion with an unfailing guarantee against pantheism, so long as Christ remains the center. "Never anywhere has any doctrine on earth brought God

---

[21] See Mouroux, *Christian Experience,* p. 12; Urs von Balthasar, "The Freedom . . . ," *loc. cit.,* p. 28; Hans Küng, "Justification and Sanctification According to the New Testament," in *Christianity Divided,* pp. 322–324.

and man so near together as Christianity. . . . Neither has any doctrine ever so carefully defended itself against the most shocking of all blasphemies, that after God had taken the step it then should be taken in vain."[22]

Jesus Christ is the final union of limited and absolute freedom. In him "the natures that are brought together into true unity are different; still, from both there is one Christ and Son; not as though the difference between the natures were taken away by their union, but rather both divinity and humanity produce the perfection of our one Lord, Christ and Son, by their inexpressible and mysterious joining into unity."[23] Every attempt of man to preserve his freedom by building a wall of security, by isolating himself from others, is bound to fail. In a world seeking freedom by the establishment of private autonomy, Jesus is the unsurpassable testimony that not only is freedom not destroyed by proximity to God, but that man is free precisely insofar as he is present to God. Jesus is the living proof that man is freedom for God.[24]

Man needs the truth to make him free, but all his grasping after bits of information does not bring him any nearer his goal. He can seek his way along many paths, some of which are reasonable and bearable if not wholly adequate. He can even discover a god of the universe. But when he meets the God of Christian revelation an ultimate acceptance or rejection is demanded of him. "The God given to man in Christ is different from any god man discovers for himself . . . God's revelation of himself in the cross is so confusing to man, so incredible, that

[22] Søren Kierkegaard, *Fear and Trembling; Sickness Unto Death* (New York, Doubleday Anchor Books, 1954), p. 248.

[23] Council of Chalcedon; translation from Clarkson *et al., The Church Teaches,* p. 167.

[24] For an expansion of these ideas, see Gabriel Moran, "Freedom in Christian Revelation," in *Proceedings: Society of Catholic College Teachers of Sacred Doctrine,* XI (1965), pp. 59–79.

he has to laugh and mock it, as long as he does not surrender his human and worldly statements."[25]

The act of faith called for here is the most perfect union of knowledge and love. It would be meaningless to ask, for example, whether St. John considers faith to be moral or intellectual. Faith for him is the entrance into a new creation, an act which establishes man in freedom and truth. In St. John's understanding of faith no isolated part of man's life is in question; God "invites man to choose for or against existence."[26] There is no neutrality in the most ultimate of questions for man. To refuse to say "yes" is already to have said "no": not to say "no" is already to have said "yes," if not to historical Christian revelation, at least to the way that leads there.[27] What is first demanded of a man is not great feats or professions of love, but to stop struggling and to receive in the passivity of receptiveness the love made visible in the person of Jesus and all who are to be his brethren.

The call of Christian revelation is the call to every man to see in the final revelation of Jesus the true way to freedom. It is a call to the acknowledgment that man's freedom has no limits to its creative possibilities if only man will surrender to the one who constitutes him in freedom. "The Church and the soul, as they receive the seed of the word and its meaning, can do nothing but await in feminine openness and readiness, not struggling or stiffening or hardening, not trying to make any masculine contribution, but simply surrendering in the dark, conceiving and bearing in the dark, not knowing what or how much has been conceived and brought to birth."[28]

[25] Schmaus, *Essence of Christianity,* p. 174.
[26] See Decourtray, *loc. cit.,* p. 571; Thomas Barrosse, "The Relationship of Love to Faith in St. John," in *Theological Studies,* XVIII (December, 1957), pp. 538–559.
[27] See Urs von Balthasar, *Science, Religion and Christianity,* p. 72.
[28] Urs von Balthasar, *Theology of History,* p. 119.

161

IX.

Revelation to All the Earth

THE subject matter of this work is the divine, supernatural revelation made by God within the experience of the church. In the previous chapter when I dealt with the individual's reception of God's revelation, I restricted my consideration to the Christian who is baptized and has the benefit of Scripture, sacraments, and the lives of other Christian people. I could not now very well stop at this point, however, but must extend the same viewpoint to include those outside of Christianity, especially the unevangelized peoples of the world. This is an important step for two reasons. In the first place, we have discovered in modern times that the unevangelized of the Christian era are not the exception but the majority of mankind. Catholic theology has not advanced a great deal on this point since St. Thomas proposed for his "man in the woods" that "God would either reveal to him through internal inspiration what had to be believed, or would send some preacher of the faith to him" (*De Ver.* XIV, 11, ad 1). But as Victor White has remarked, "we know of many millions more men in different sorts of woods than St. Thomas ever imagined."[1] Second, if the case of the unevangelized is not the exception to which God supplies an *ad hoc* solution, it may throw light upon the Christian life as well. "If a man is saved in ignorance of the Christian message then what happens in his heart must be essentially identical with the justification

[1] White, *loc. cit.*, p. 32.

162

of the Christian. Any other position, it seems to me, would be heretical. Even the man who is saved apart from the Christian message is justified by faith and baptism."[2]

The supposition of a "primitive revelation" in the naïve form in which it was put forth in an earlier century is hardly credible today.[3] Catholic theology, however, continues to insist that man achieves salvation only in the assent to God supernaturally revealed. The reduction of the number of supernatural truths that would be of minimum necessity for salvation does not come to grips with the real problem which is how a supernatural revelation plays any part at all in the "good pagan's" life. The doctrine of "baptism of desire" as the means to salvation is a statement of the question rather than the answer.

If we were to accept only what the earlier treatises have said on revelation, there would seem little possibility of relating revelation to the unevangelized except by positing a special divine intervention to supply it. On the other hand, the more extensive development of a theology of revelation that we have seen in contemporary Catholic writing has within itself the principles of a solution to this question. This answer is a highly significant one not only in speculative theories on God's salvific will, but also in the immediate practical problems of missionary work and catechetical procedure.

REVELATION AND THE UNEVANGELIZED

We may take note first of all that Catholic belief predicates a "natural revelation of God" in the universe, that is, the possibility of knowing God by the light of reason. "The same holy Mother Church holds and teaches that God, the origin and end of all

[2] Gregory Baum, " 'Honest to God' and Traditional Theology," in *Ecumenist,* II (May, 1964), p. 67.

[3] See Wilhelm Schmidt, *Primitive Revelation* (St. Louis, B. Herder, 1939), pp. 1–41; Karl Rahner, *Offenbarung und Uberlieferung* (Freiburg, Herder, 1965), p. 17; Charles Davis, *Theology for Today* (New York, Sheed and Ward, 1962), p. 117.

things, can be known with certainty by the natural light of human reason from the things that he created."[4] A thorough analysis of this Vatican I text need not be attempted here. We may say, however, that a radical split of nature and supernature, faith and reason, cannot be justified on the basis of the Church's definition. The First Vatican Council made no claims for any system of proofs from reason, no demands for a full-blown natural theology as a preparation for Christian faith.

The assumption of many Catholic treatises that it is possible, not to say desirable, to bracket supernatural revelation and faith while one constructs rational proofs about God, is a highly doubtful premise. The fact that a man is a believer raises some important problems when he begins to philosophize. Whatever solutions may be proposed, it would seem that the one thing that a believer cannot do is pretend that he is not a believer and then face the philosophical questions with openness and honesty.[5] Treatises in which God's existence and attributes are worked out *more geometrico* previous to any question of faith would seem to constitute an unnecessary barrier to dialogue with those outside the Catholic faith. It is one thing for medieval theologians to speculate on the rational bases of faith; it is quite another thing for us to brandish their arguments in modern controversies while pretending to abstract from all contexts of faith. The misunderstanding of arguments torn from a theological setting to be literally repeated in a work of rational apologetics is a fault from which we have not yet fully escaped.[6]

The chief concern of the Church's magisterium has been to safeguard what holy Scripture implies throughout its teaching,

---

[4] Translation from Clarkson *et al., The Church Teaches,* p. 27.

[5] Pieper, *Leisure . . . ,* pp. 147–166; L. Malevez, "The Believer and the Philosopher," in *Philosophy Today,* V (Spring, 1961), pp. 14–30.

[6] Perhaps the most serious misrepresentation is that of the "ontological argument" of St. Anselm which continues to be ripped from its faith context despite the painstaking analysis of Karl Barth, *Anselm: Fides Quaerens Intellectum* (Richmond, John Knox, 1960).

namely, that man's belief is not an irrational leap, but is supported by man's God-given nature which already has some contact with God. "Precisely so that Revelation might be grace, it is necessary at least in principle that man should have something to do with God from a locus which is not already grace."[7] The teaching of St. Paul in Romans 1 and 2 implies some kind of natural revelation of God through the universe and through man's moral experience. More important than this explicit mentioning of a natural revelation being possible is the presupposition of both the Old and the New Testament that there is no need to prove God's existence because the universe is sufficient testimony for anyone with an open mind and a docile heart. The message of the Bible, therefore, was not that there was a god, but that God had spoken to Israel and the Church, that he was still present with his people and calling them to a more intimate relation with himself. Not to have heard him speak and therefore to worship him unknowingly was understandable (Acts 17:16–31); not to have recognized him as existing was unexcusable (Wis. 13:1; Rom. 1:17–20).

The problem of the unevangelized, however, is not resolved by this so-called natural or general revelation of God. The teaching of the Church is that salvation comes through Christ, that is, through a sharing in the revelation that takes place in the consciousness of the risen Lord and is mediated to the world through Church and gospel. This is the heart of the question which needs further examination.

According to Catholic belief, God has established for man an end that gives absolute completion to his nature. God's decree

---

[7] Rahner, "Current Problems . . . ," *loc. cit.*, p. 183; see also *Constitution on Divine Revelation,* Chapter I, Article 3, and William Temple, *Nature, Man and God* (London, Macmillan, 1935), p. 306: "Only if God is revealed in the rising of the sun in the sky can He be revealed in the rising of a son of man from the dead; only if He is revealed in the history of Syrians and Philistines can He be revealed in the history of Israel; only if He chooses all men for His own can He choose any at all; only if nothing is profane can anything be sacred."

of man's end is not merely a moral or juridical entity that could enter man's experience only by someone informing him of it. If the natural and supernatural are not simply juxtaposed externally, man's nature cannot remain unaffected by the fact that he is living in a supernatural order and that God wills no other end for him than a share in the life of the Trinity.[8] The call of God has been realized in the incarnation such that the attainment of the end is not just a possibility but has actually been accomplished, even though the individual must ratify this by his free decision. In Christ's life and more definitively in his death-resurrection, all of humanity has been assumed into a new relation with God.

The experience which man now has of his own person is not the same as it would have been in a state of pure nature. Long before the fact of a supernatural order is brought before him as objective knowledge, he has already taken up a position with reference to it because it is a "given" of his concrete, personal structure. There is a remarkable passage in St. Thomas in which he says that, at the age of reason, "the first thing that occurs to a man to think about then, is to deliberate about himself. And if he then direct himself to the due end, he will, by means of grace, receive the remission of original sin; whereas if he does not then direct himself to the due end, as far as he is capable of discretion at that particular age, he will sin mortally, through not doing that which is in his power to do."[9] Whatever precisions we would make on this "age of reason," there is a way indicated here which has reference to all people including the unevangelized. St. Thomas is suggesting that every person is faced with the Christian mystery of revelation in terms which

---

8 See Louis Malevez, "La gratuité du surnaturel," in *Nouvelle revue théologique*, LXXXV (1953), pp. 561–586; Karl Rahner, "Concerning the Relationship between Nature and Grace," *Theological Investigations*, vol. I, pp. 297–317; J. P. Kenny, "Reflections on Human Nature and the Supernatural," in *Theological Studies*, XIV (March, 1953), pp. 280–287.

9 *S.T.* Ia-IIae, q. 89, a. 6, c.

are connatural to him prior to any scriptural or doctrinal instruction.[10]

Man does not stand neutral before God; he must take a position for or against his end which is in fact supernatural. The unevangelized man who seeks God, who holds himself open to the possible revelation of God, who ratifies the entelechy of his concrete existence by moral decisions, has already experienced God's revelation and has already accepted God's grace. The "signs of revelation" for such a man are the conditions of his own moral life: his weaknesses, his struggling, his ideals which in fact go beyond the purely human. He meets God at those hard edges of experience which can never be transmuted into an extension of himself.

In the context of a supernaturally oriented existence, the most ordinary actions of man's life bear a dimension which is more than natural. Above all, however, in the profound human experiences of trust and love, fidelity and courage, suffering and death, there emerges a relation to an absolute ideal beyond the human even though the individual's expression of it may be badly distorted or poorly articulated.[11] Here God's grace is at work and here God's revelation in Christ is experienced albeit implicitly. What must not be forgotten by the Christian, therefore, is that those who have never heard of an historical revelation may achieve a more genuine repentance, humility, and sanctity than those who have. The Christian has no reason for pride; he has been chosen not on the basis of merit, but in order to serve as God's witness in bringing to explicit conscious-

[10] See Dulles, *loc. cit.,* p. 52.

[11] See Karl Rahner, "Christianity and Non-Christian Religions," in *The Church. Readings in Theology,* compiled at the Canisianum (New York, P. J. Kenedy and Sons, 1963), pp. 131–132; Urs von Balthasar, *Word and Redemption,* p. 43: "Everything in the created order, with the exception of sin, is enabled through Christ, to be an expression of God, most of all what we would think to be most remote from him: the cross, opprobrium, anguish, death."

ness what has already been accomplished or is being accomplished by God's grace.

This experience of God's revelation which occurs in man's decision regarding his own person is never an isolated act. We have already pointed out the social character of human life as reflected in knowledge, thought, and language. There is a constant interchange between men that modern civilization has increased in astounding proportions. As man's influence spreads outward from human relationships, the objective patterns of nature take on the impress of man. The whole social structure becomes the medium of communication between men and a dominant influence in the life of the individual. The more complex society becomes, the more does the world appear as man's world—for better or for worse. The anonymous order of the nonpersonal structure ceases to be morally neutral or of negligible concern.[12] God has redeemed man in his entirety, in the sociability of his nature, and in the "worldliness" of his concerns. By taking hold of man, the Spirit necessarily took hold of man's world (Rom. 8:19–23). There is a difference, of course, in the degree or kind of revelation that can be mediated by various objects and events in the universe, but the central and indispensable element in every revelatory situation is man, the recipient to whom God addresses himself.

Each man, therefore, stands before God with all of mankind and the whole of his earthly circumstances. In finding the God of supernatural revelation (or in letting himself be found), each man does not have to start *ab ovo* with some private, inner religious experience. Each man dwells in a world oriented in some way to God revealed in Christ. Man's saving act of faith through the revelatory experience of God is mediated by the concrete details of his own terrestrial circumstances. Nothing of itself is guaranteed to be revelatory of God, but everything by

[12] See Remy C. Kwant, *Encounter* (Pittsburgh, Duquesne University, 1960), p. 72.

the grace of God is capable of becoming a revelatory instrument. This principle would seem to be of the utmost importance in any pastoral consideration, but it is a principle, unfortunately, which has not been applied with all seriousness in Catholic theology and practice.

If the social structure in general is capable of entering into the revelatory experience of men, then evidently the religion which men profess can also embody elements of an objectified revelation. God takes men into a relationship of supernatural revelation; he uses the milieu in which men actually live, and this includes the religion actually at their disposal. Catholicism cannot judge other religions to be solely the work of the devil or solely the work of man. Intermingled with the ignorance and failure of human frailty are supernatural moments of grace embedded in the religious structures. These elements are the work of great religious leaders whose accomplishments help in turn to form other religious men. Religions undoubtedly vary greatly in their capability of bringing about a genuine relation to God, but precisely which elements are authentic and which are corruptive is not always easy to determine. What does need unequivocal affirmation today is that non-Christian religious experience can bear within itself a genuine though obscured supernatural revelation; that non-Christians are saved not simply in spite of their religion, but by means of their religion insofar as it is a preparatory stage for a definitive revelation; that other great world religions must be part of God's salvific activity and are therefore to be respected and preserved until a better revelation can emerge from these peoples' lives before God.[13]

13 See *Constitution on the Church,* Chapter II, Article 16; see also S. T. Balasuriya, "Toward a Wider Ecumenism," in *Ecumenist,* III (January, 1965), p. 24: "We may and must say that the people who are born into the religious and social environment of these religions receive through them a message of hope and life. God who has taken hold of the people in Christ may lead them in this way to actualize the kingdom in their heart, at least to some extent."

169

The foregoing thesis has nothing to do with a bland universalism or religious indifferentism. The Church and every Christian is called as missionary and servant to a world which longs to hear (even though implicitly) the word of the gospel. To this non-Christian world the Church speaks the words which Paul once spoke in Athens: "What you already worship in ignorance, that I am now telling you of" (Acts 17:23). The conviction of the apostolic Church that she was speaking to a world that was not entirely ignorant of the Christian God did not dampen the apostolic zeal of her preachers and missionaries. The word had to be preached because "this concealed knowledge of God only becomes really conscious of itself when it breaks through men's hardness of heart and is released by the Word of the God who reveals himself as utterly beyond the world."[14] A man cannot form someone else into a Christian, but he can expose the other to the light which can help him to reflect upon the grace-filled depths of his own existence and that of his brothers. Those who do enter the Christian Church, who explicitly affirm their faith in the God of Jesus Christ, have already been living in the anonymous Christian sphere.

Year by year the influence of world-wide communications and the growth in the complexity of society make this objectified and inchoate revelation more of a force to be reckoned with. Objective elements from revelation have become diffused over the world and embedded in the structure of society. There is today practically no one to whom Christianity can deliver the message completely anew. Christianity must acknowledge the possibility of learning something of herself from other religions. With all men and with all religions the Church today must enter into dialogue.[15]

[14] Karl Rahner, "Theos in the New Testament," *Theological Investigations*, vol. I, p. 98.

[15] See *Declaration on the Relation of the Church to Non-Christian Religions*, Article 2.

OBJECTIVE AND SUBJECTIVE IN
REVELATIONAL HISTORY

What I have posited above and what I have many times asserted or implied is that revelation has its foundation in the Trinitarian relations which encompass man even before he is conscious of God's action. This raises a question concerning the most fundamental dichotomy that has dominated modern thought, namely, the subject-object schema. Is revelation primarily something objective (doctrines, historical events, persons) or is it primarily subjective (interior light, attraction of grace, inner testimony)?

In the analysis of revelation there has been a continuing oscillation between these two poles, an emphasis upon one followed by a reaction to the other. Latourelle, after outlining the modern treatment of revelation as a movement from emphasis *ex parte objecti* to *ex parte potentiae*, says of the present: "Contemporary theology does not want to lose any of the aspects but to harmonize them in a unity, for revelation is at once action, event, history, knowledge, witness, encounter, doctrine, unchanging deposit, interior word."[16] Latourelle is no doubt right in saying that this is what contemporary theology is trying to maintain. However, simply to say that revelation is all of these things is not thereby to succeed in understanding it as a unity, or to overcome the difficulties that continually cause the split. The separation of these elements and the exaggerated emphasis upon some of them continues to occur. My thesis would be that revelation can be none of these things unless fundamentally it is something other than any or all of them.

Catholic treatises which are aware of the complexity of the problem try to strike a balance between the objective and subjective. Writers of these works are usually quite confident of their accuracy and orthodoxy because they have not left out

16 Latourelle, *op. cit.*, p. 257.

anything. They have not fallen into the subjectivist error of many heretics, nor have they neglected the subjective element. On the one hand, therefore, there is the "revealed truth," the object of faith. But there must also be an inner light of faith, an interior testimony (which is sometimes called revelation, too). This duality would seem to take into account the whole process: "A sort of interior revelation must be added to the revelation which strikes our ears, if we are to believe."[17]

Surely the correct procedure for Catholic theology is to insist upon both of these aspects. But the solution comes so quickly and so easily that one is led to suspect that the question has not been seriously raised or understood. What is wrong with the common attempt to steer a middle course between subjectivism and objectivism is that it is much more a restatement of the question than it is an answer to the question. The history of theories of revelation is not the history of subjectivists and objectivists, but the history of those who tried to steer a middle course between subjectivism and objectivism, and much to their dismay found themselves accused of one or the other. It might be that this has continually happened not because the middle way was not carefully steered, but because the middle way does not exist. On this point I find myself forced to agree with Brunner: "There is no right middle way between objectivism and subjectivism: there is no mean between two errors. . . . The Bible is as little concerned with objective as with subjective truth. The objective-subjective antithesis cannot be applied to the Word of God."[18]

Catholic theology, I have said, generally claims to achieve a balance between the subjective and objective. In fact, however, what has held sway for the greater part of recent centuries has been a highly objectified notion of revelation. Even at present, whatever is said about the necessity of a subjective light of faith,

[17] Joly, *op. cit.*, p. 122.
[18] Brunner, *Truth as Encounter*, p. 84.

it is clearly the object, what is delivered to man from the outside, that is called revelation without hesitation or qualification. Modernism arose in Catholic circles partly as a protest against an objectified, impersonal, non-historical revelation. By simply reacting to what was wrong and not getting to the root of the problem, modernists tried to substitute an "inner experience" for an "outer object." This conception of revelation was completely inadequate to the richness of revelation and so modernism was forthrightly condemned.[19]

In opposition to the modernist trend, more stress than before was laid upon the objective elements (especially the teachings of the Church and of theologians) in the revelational process. Recent attempts to make faith more meaningful by describing it as commitment or encounter are still vitiated by a definite bias for the objective side when it comes to stating, or more often implying, what revelation is. Contemporary theology's concern with the revelatory events in Israelite history, as well as its assertion that Christ is the revelation, do not in themselves overcome and may even strengthen this objectivist assumption.

In attempting to show how the non-evangelized participate in God's revelation, it might seem that I have merely reverted to a subjectivistic notion of revelation. This I would deny just as I deny that the juxtaposition of objective and subjective elements is any solution to the problem. A deeper unity than that of subject and object must be reached or else these opposing elements cannot be held together. It is thoroughly impossible in a work of this kind to carry through such a program. I do hope, however, that this work succeeds in pointing to the question and the need for Catholic theology to make more use of the philosophical study in this century which has in fact largely gravitated around this problem.

The radical split introduced by Cartesian philosophy domi-

19 For the development of the notion of revelation after the modernist crisis, see Rahner, *Offenbarung . . . ,* pp. 11ff.

nated centuries of philosophical thought and still influences today both philosophy and the "common-sense" notion of knowledge. The problem was not of Descartes' creation in that this dichotomy was almost certain to arise with reflexive and systematic concentration upon human thought. What was needed was a deeper understanding of man in relation to being. Much of recent philosophy has been an attempt to overcome the subject-object split by returning to a more primordial ground of unity in man's "being-in-the world," to a pre-predicative relation of man and being. Catholic philosophers and theologians, aided by the present philosophical context, have also been recovering in the best of Catholic tradition a foundation which precedes the subject-object dichotomy.[20] In Aquinas's ontology of knowledge, the split between subject and object is not the fundamental characteristic of knowledge. The basic relationship is that which constitutes a subject in being and relates subjects to one another. The affirmation of particular objective facts unfolds within the prior relationship which establishes the subject in the truth. The main problem for Aquinas is never that of bridging the gap between subject and object, but of explaining how such a gap is possible.[21] An adequate theology of revelation needs a metaphysics that is capable of dealing with such foundational questions and is at the same time open to enrichment by the phenomenological and personalist studies of the present.

[20] It should be noted that the words subject and object have quite different meanings in contemporary thought as compared to medieval theology. We must be careful not to read distortions or dichotomies into an earlier period on the basis of terminology alone. Neither can one find the answer to the subject-object dichotomy plainly stated in Aquinas since the question was never raised in those terms; on this point, see Frederick Wilhelmsen, *The Metaphysics of Love* (New York, Sheed and Ward, 1962), p. 27; Jacques Maritain, *Existence and the Existent* (Garden City, Doubleday Image Books, 1956), pp. 70–91.

[21] See Rahner, *Geist in Welt*, p. 88; see also Finance, *loc. cit.*; Robert Johann, "Subjectivity," *Review of Metaphysics*, XII (1958), pp. 200–234.

God's revelation does not stand outside man as an object to be known by a special inner light. Even less than everything else in man's experience is God not juxtaposed as a thing "outside" man; but neither is he "inside" man. He precedes the distinction of inner and outer. It is only as a consequence of God's indwelling (which is not to be confused with being located in a container) that there arises an inner light of faith and an outer mediating object. Neither the one nor the other nor the two together is the revelation. They are instead the symbolic expressions of a revelation which both causes and is affected by this inner-outer manifestation. The objective or outer element is primarily the human bodily activity (for example, the speaking of words, the eating of the Eucharist), but also includes beyond man the non-personal sphere of books, institutions, and sacramental objects. These do not cease to be revelatory instruments, but they retain their revelatory meaning only because they are involved in the total process of God speaking to man in the very ground of his freedom-knowledge.

The study of God's "indwelling" therefore, is not one peripheral question in theology, but the center of theology, the rediscovery of what the Bible and the great theologians have said of the relation of God and man. God lives among his people in the intimacy of a person-to-person relation, in the exchange of knowledge through gestures of love that penetrates to the heart of man. Where there is revelation there is a participating subject in a community who experiences God's presence at a deeper level than that of objective consciousness and who responds to the revelatory bestowal in bodily symbols of love and worship. This union of the human spirit with subsistent Truth is not the intrusion of a foreign body into man, but the growing of man into the likeness of God, which man discovers is at the same time a growing into his own true self, a deepening and integration of the being he was given at creation.

From what we have said in this chapter it becomes evident

175

that the revelational history may involve the most diverse objects and external events. The Church as the hierarchically structured community of believers and the Scripture as the literary precipitate of the Church's consciousness have an unsurpassable and indefectible role to play within this history. Nevertheless, though the Spirit testifies to the Son, men do not always hear and follow out the designs of God. Through ignorance, weakness, or malice the revelation can find expression in men in ways which are partially at variance with the gospel or the life and teaching of the visible Church. "When it is a question for an unbeliever, of attaining the supernatural God of revelation by means of images and concepts made for something quite different, we can see that there will sometimes be a disproportion—and a great one at that—between his conceptual material and his spiritual thought, between what he represents to himself and what he affirms."[22] Thus what may at the level of objective expression be opposed to the Church's interpretive norms might yet be part of the revelational process. Certainly, our criteria and our norms give us some basis for distinguishing between events that belong to a sacred history and those of profane history. In practice, however, it is not man's prerogative to know with certainty whether a particular event is part of God's revelatory intercourse with man.

It is not difficult to state very general principles. We know that the history of Israel, at least in the major events that the Bible records, was part of God's plan to prepare for his Son. We know, too, that the history of the Church is the privileged witness of God's continuing revelation. The mighty works of Israel and the Church are part of a special revelational history that is to be distinguished from the general relation of God and his creation.

We must go further than this, however. Even in the Old Testament there were glimpses of the fact that God's special

[22] Mouroux, *I Believe,* p. 73.

relation to Israel was not an isolated part of creation. A Noachian covenant preceded Israel, and creation itself was oriented toward the covenant relation. Israel was the guarantee of a sacred history that went beyond the boundaries of Israel. The one chosen by God is not taken as a substitute for the others, but as the representative who in some way includes the others. In Israel's case, she was the chosen representative for a mission which concerned all the nations. The Fathers of the Church were not wholly wrong in their belief that there was a Gentile salvation history.[23] The historical cultures which surrounded Israel, all of the religion and philosophy of the ancient world, cannot be dismissed as only incidentally juxtaposed to Israel's history. In the light of later developments we can see more clearly that all of humanity was being called to a communion in grace, and this means that the revelational history which prepared for Jesus Christ has roots also in other peoples besides the Jews.

What is true of the nations before Christ is all the more true of people in the eschatological period after him. All creation receives God's redeeming grace, and there can be no doubt that all are called to the intimacy of his own divine life. The ultimate meaning of profane history is thus locked in the history of Christ and his Church, for this Church is the "historically visible vanguard—the historically and socially constituted expression of that which the Christian knows to exist as a hidden reality even outside the visibility of the Church."[24] Although secular history cannot be immediately identified with the continuing revelational history, it is history that is eventually to be the *pleroma* of Christ's victory. The people of God that is to be co-extensive with all the peoples of mankind is eventually to be taken up into the gospel to reveal its full meaning. A dialectic of revelation and human culture continues throughout the whole

---

[23] See Urs von Balthasar, *Word and Revelation,* p. 54.
[24] Rahner, "Christianity and . . . ," *loc. cit.,* p. 133.

period and always involves some tensions and conflicts that are not immediately resolvable.[25] The ultimate indivisibility of sacred and profane history will become evident only from the perspective of the final judgment.

[25]See Dondeyne, *Faith and the Modern World,* pp. 121–125; Jean Daniélou, *The Salvation of the Nations* (Notre Dame, University of Notre Dame, 1962), p. 106; Karl Rahner, "Weltgeschichte und Heilsgeschichte," in *Schriften* . . . . Band V, pp. 115–135; Edward Schillebeeckx, "The Church and Mankind," in *The Church and Mankind,* edited Edward Schillebeeckx and Karl Rahner (New York, Paulist Press, 1965), pp. 69–102.

X.

Revelation in Heaven

CONCERNING the consummation of man's life in heaven there is very little that man can say. St. Paul spoke mostly in negative terms when trying to give an indication of those things "which no eye ever saw and no ears heard, and never occurred to the human mind" (1 Cor. 2:9). Christ spoke of man's life with God in terms of images (kingdom, banquet, mansions) which provide some insight while not satisfying at all our curiosity. Medieval and modern theology has spoken of a "beatific vision," an image which many people find not especially meaningful or compelling. For our present purpose, however, there are a few important points that are raised in Scripture and theology on the relation of revelation to man's last end. My intention here is not merely to round off the discussion with a conclusion, but to throw additional light on some of the previous material. I shall center the chapter around two points: 1) faith and glory 2) Christ as eternal mediator.

FAITH AND GLORY

The Christian life is the acceptance of God's self-gift to man in faith. The participation in revelation grows ever deeper in proportion to man's receptivity before God. This relationship was accomplished in a plan of God worked out in human

179

history. With the coming of Christ and his entrance into glory, the definitive stage of that plan was reached. To believe in God revealed in Christ is to share in that glory of the last days. He who believes in the Son already possesses eternal life.

St. John's gospel is most striking in showing faith on earth as not merely preparatory to but as the present possession of eternal life. Revelation has reached a high point never to be diminished; in entering the revelatory relationship man enters eternal life. Thus, heaven is not an object bestowed upon man to reward him for doing good things in his life. Heaven is rather the full-flowering of a life now being lived on earth. "At the moment of the disappearance of the last trace of self-love," writes Schillebeeckx, "the beatific vision wells up spontaneously as if from within, in our very being purified by grace, as if the bursting open of the bubble of self-love made visible the deepest reality of the true I."[1] Patristic and medieval treatments of faith retained this central insight that "faith is a habit of mind, whereby eternal life is begun in us."[2] Likewise, the Council of Trent was far removed from an extrinsicist and objectified picture of faith and salvation in speaking of faith as "the beginning of man's salvation, the foundation and source of all justification."[3]

Although the last age has begun, the glory of God has been manifested in Christ Jesus, and the Spirit has been poured out upon the earth, there is nevertheless another side to Christian revelation. At first sight this latter side that we now speak of may seem sharply opposed to the former. In fact, however, these two aspects of revelation complement each other, even though they coexist in some tension.

The Bible presents Christian revelation as the final stage of

[1] Edward Schillebeeckx, "The Death of a Christian," in *The Layman in the Church* (New York, Alba House, 1963), p. 77.

[2] *S.T.* IIa-IIae, q. 4, a. 1, c.

[3] Translation from Clarkson *et al.*, *The Church Teaches*, p. 235; see Aubert, *op. cit.*, p. 787.

God's communication with man, but it is no less evident in the Bible that there is a revelation to come. This revelation is already given in principle, but is still hidden by our earthly condition. St. Paul especially brings out this perspective on revelation. He looks forward to the revelation when the Lord shall appear in glory. Paul, and with him the later Christian, is "waiting for our Lord Jesus Christ to reappear" (1 Cor. 1:7). The glory is to be revealed from on high, and then we shall see face to face (1 Cor. 13:12; 2 Thes. 1:7). St. John, particularly in his epistles, rejoins St. Paul on this view of a revelation still to come when "we shall be like him, for we shall see him as he is" (1 Jn. 3:2). In the final book of the Bible the word "revelation" (or "apocalypse") comes to refer chiefly to what is still to be revealed in the future. The Church's life is shaped by this future kingdom; the Church is a harbinger of a reality breaking into history from the future.

If revelation were naïvely conceived to be a collection of truths stored in apostolic writings, this latter aspect of revelation to which Scripture clearly testifies would be inexplicable. If, on the other hand, revelation is the intersubjective experience of God and the human community brought to full intensity in the God-man and being brought to participated perfection in the rest of men, then obviously revelation has both a present and a future aspect.

Not only will revelation happen in the future; by its very nature it can never cease. The revelation on earth is to be completed by the revelation in heaven. Between two persons (at least when one or both are human) there is no deeper communion than a revelatory one, that is, a continuing and free, giving and receiving of personal knowledge.

The word "vision" is not entirely satisfactory for describing the full living of revelation. It could easily give the impression of a looking upon an object, but this is almost the exact opposite of what is intended by the term "beatific vision." If the word "vision" is used at all, it must be understood not as the replacement of revelation, but as the perfection of revelation in an intimacy and intensity not possible on earth. I would therefore question the usual terminology of Catholic treatises which speak of revelation being completed or replaced by vision of God. The word "revelation" would be better used to cover the whole process. Revelation is to be neither completed nor replaced. Instead, man, living in revelatory relationship with God by the light of faith, is to find his fulfillment in the revelatory experience of heaven by the light of glory. Some German authors distinguish a *Wortoffenbarung* and *Schauoffenbarung,* which, if applied to this question, has the advantage of making *Offenbarung* the continuing element. This could still suffer, however, from too sharp a contrast between *Wort* and *Schau.* Any implication of passing from a revelation which is "listened to" to a revelation which is "looked at" must be carefully avoided. Whatever objective elements may enter the process, revelation from the Christian viewpoint is at every stage of development the participation of man within a community in the self-bestowing love of God made full in Jesus Christ.

The passing of the theological virtue of faith, as St. Paul describes it in 1 Corinthians 13, is not the replacement of *pistis* with *gnosis.* It is instead the final perfection of *pistis* as imitation of the Son's fidelity to the Father. Man never takes possession of the object of his "vision." He remains like the Son eternally obedient and receptive.[4] The earthly faith which passes does not simply cease; it makes way for an adult knowledge in the same manner in which a child's knowledge gives way to maturity. Waiting in hope and faith for the coming of God is not a filling in of time, but a time of being filled with God. Those who have concerned themselves with truth and love will have their hunger satisfied. "Faith becomes in me a power whose vital intellectual

[4] See Urs von Balthasar, *Theology of History,* p. 40; Durrwell, *Resurrection,* p. 355.

force is gripped by an almost biological hunger for fulfillment—for that beatific vision of God, of which faith is the earthly bait."[5]

St. Thomas describes the beatific vision by saying that God is known by man without the medium of an intellectual *species*. This means that the heavenly experience of God is not mediated by the objective elements always present in our other knowledge of things and people. The revelatory relation of God and man, which already in this life is one of subject to subject, is in heaven brought to unimaginable perfection. "This union is consummated in act through the *lumen gloriae*, which is nothing but the *terminus ad extra* of the divine eternal intention. It is a union of person to person as creature and Creator can unite, and it is the final consummation in the creature of his presence to God from all eternity, so that now at last he can know God as God in Christ has known him. (Phil. 3:12)."[6]

The gift of Uncreated Act by the power of the Spirit is already made to man on earth and issues in the life of grace and the cognitive aspect of this grace, the consciously participated revelation. At the end of man's terrestrial stay, the Spirit is still the principle of knowledge, but now freed from the weight of man's earthly selfishness, the Spirit's activity issues in a far more intimate relation.[7] Man lives with the life of the Trinity in a fascinating communion of loving knowledge.

The one danger present in this description of the beatific vision is that the Spirit has taken man to such an extent that there is no longer a distinction between man and God. This is an objection not lightly to be dismissed; it is not answered simply by asserting that there is a distinction. We would, in fact,

[5] Chenu, *op. cit.,* p. 30.

[6] David Burrell, "Indwelling: Presence and Dialogue," in *Theological Studies,* XXII (March, 1961), p. 14.

[7] See Karl Rahner, "Some Implications of the Scholastic Concept of Uncreated Grace," in *Theological Investigations,* vol. I, pp. 326–340.

be hard put to escape all tinge of pantheism if it were not for one fact: Jesus, our eternal mediator of revelation.

ETERNAL REVELATION IN CHRIST

The final norm of whether a truly Christological understanding of revelation has been attained is the place that Christ holds in the heavenly revelation. Until recently, the tracts *De Novissimis* gave little indication of any place to a Christ-relation in heaven other than as a source of "accidental joy." However, a number of authors in the last few years have brought out the role of Christ in the "beatific vision." They have also shown that this point is of no little significance for theology.

It remains eternally true that no one sees the Father except the Son and he to whom the Son reveals.[8] Christ will not abandon the function of cornerstone. He will not cease to be the head and the life-giving principle of his Church. The lamb will be the eternal light of knowledge in whom God reveals himself. "The city does not need the sun nor the moon to shine in it, for the glory of God lighted it, and the Lamb is its lamp" (Apoc. 21:23).

If this mediatorial role of Christ in the beatific vision seems to conflict with our previous insistence that we know God in the closest possible intimacy, then we really have not understood what is meant by saying that Christ is the revelation.[9] If Christ were only the one through whom God spoke, the object in which revelation was summed up, the man Jesus would be an obstacle to the most direct vision of God. But, as we have said repeatedly throughout this work, Christ is not God presented as an object to human eyes. Christ is rather the revelatory communion itself: both the giving of the Father to the world and the reception and response of man. The fullness of revelation is found in the consciousness of the glorified Lord; it is toward

---

[8] See Rahner, "Die ewige . . . ," *loc. cit.,* p. 58.
[9] See Alfaro, "Cristo glorioso . . . ," *loc. cit.,* pp. 62–63.

union with that consciousness that the Church is moving. Christ, as the second Adam and as head of the world-wide Church, received at his death-resurrection the revelatory experience for all mankind. To the degree that men are united with that humanity they share in the subjective consciousness of Christ who lives in face to face communion with the Father. His humanity was the one way to the Father; it remains so today; it will remain so for eternity. "The way invites them to walk on it and pursue it to the end. Christ takes them by the hand, as it were, and leads them to the Father."[10]

To know God in Christ is not, therefore, to know indirectly. Simply to look upon God would be an indirect way of knowing mediated by the objective order. On the other hand, to share with Christ the exchange of life between Father and Son is "to know" with the deepest possible intimacy. "It will be a complete cognitive experience, we shall see face to face (1 Cor. 13:12), we shall live in the vision of the Lord (2 Cor. 5:7), and this must surely be because then our living union in love will be complete. Since the love of the Spirit is the root of knowledge on earth, it will surely be in the Spirit that the knowledge of heaven will enlighten us."[11]

The eternal revelational communion in Jesus also shows why the "beatific vision" is a communal activity and an act of man's bodily nature. If heaven were naïvely imagined as a looking at God, it would obviously be conceived as an individualistic activity. It was not by accident that medieval theology's conception of a "vision of God by separated souls" came to the forefront concomitant with an obscuring of the historical and social nature of Christian revelation. This awareness of the historical and social in the revelation of earth and heaven is of the utmost importance pastorally. The failure to understand this central aspect of revelation is best seen in the inadequate de-

10 Schmaus, *Essence of Christianity,* p. 265.
11 Durrwell, *Resurrection,* p. 255.

velopment of a theology of hope. When the historical and social dimensions of revelation were obscured, hope became quite secondary in significance. Hope came to be directed vertically out of history, and theologians generally taught that one could properly hope for oneself but not for others. The two marks which distinguish a Christian hope were precisely what had been lost.[12]

If, however, the beatific vision is a communion in Christ, it is possible only with and through other men who are united to Christ. The Body of Christ is being formed on earth with an historical and social hope as its driving power. The building of a human community based upon the principles of Christ's love thus becomes the direct preparation for the beatific vision. The whole world flows into Christ's resurrection and the transformation of his Body. We cannot know for certain just how this world is to be perfected into his Body, but we do know that when this perfection is reached, all things will be man's, and man will be Christ's, and Christ will be God's. We can see here why the Eucharist is called the foretaste of heaven. In eucharistic celebration and communion all men are united in Christ their eldest brother in his going to the Father. This structure that is expressed in earthly symbol is exactly the same as that of the beatific vision.

The "resurrection of the body" is not an afterthought which adds an accidental pleasure to the main joy of seeing God. Whatever be the state of man's existence prior to the resurrection,[13] we know that the perfection of revelation is found at that point where, bodily and socially sharing life with his

[12] See Gabriel Moran, "Hope: Foundation of Religious Education," in *Catholic Educational Review*, LXI (May, 1963), pp. 302–312; Bernard Olivier, *Christian Hope* (Westminster, Newman, 1963), pp. 50–90.

[13] I leave open the question of whether the resurrection may in some sense begin with man's death; on the questions surrounding this point, see Rahner, *On the Theology of Death;* Ladislaus Boros, *The Mystery of Death* (New York, Herder and Herder, 1965), pp. 141–165.

brothers in Christ, *man* lives in communion with the Trinity. The Parousia will be that moment at which flesh will be entirely transformed by the Spirit and man's bodily nature will be transfused with the freedom of the sons of God. The joys and pleasures of man's bodily life will be swept up into the social existence of heaven.[14]

The constant failure of non-Christian religions and Christian heresies has been to seek God by escaping from the bodily and historical condition of man. Christianity demands something less and something more than this. On the one hand, it demands not the suppression of the bodily, but the perfection of all that is bodily and human. On the other hand, Christianity demands not only a suppression but a death, and the death is not merely to man's body, but to man in his root selfishness. The death, in other words, is not to be effected through the stagnation of a Manichaean asceticism, but by a more radical submission of all that is individualistic to the community being molded in the Lord. "If anyone tries to die to himself in any other way than living by Christ in glory, he will merely succeed in establishing in himself the rule of the flesh."[15] Christian revelation is the final approbation of a purified bodily, historical, and social existence into the very life of the Trinity.

There is a sense in which history will cease, that is, the year by year totaling of time between creation and Parousia. In a more important sense of history, that is, the creation of life and meaning in the intercommunion of persons, history can never come to an end. It is impossible to conceive of a human life which would not be a never ending movement of the creature into the life of God, an everlasting advance into the incomprehensible truth and love of God. Every person is a mystery with whom we can always grow into a deeper revelational com-

14 See Karl Rahner, "The Resurrection of the Body," *Theological Investigations*, vol. II, pp. 212–214.
15 Durrwell, *Resurrection*, p. 348.

munion of knowledge. But it is our very inability to give or to receive in entirety that makes us grow weary of human relationships. God is the mystery whose communion of grace does not weary us; he is the fulfillment of man's desires and yet he always remains incomprehensible. "Having supremely revealed the character of his mystery as grace in the abandonment of his Son during the time of our mortality, he will reveal it to our bliss in eternity."[16]

Man's entrance into final communion is at once, the realization of the perfection of man and the glorification of God. Man discovers that he becomes himself in his union with the Son and as adopted son. The total receptivity demanded of a son is the way in which the creature "gives glory." It is not by offering external objects that he glorifies God, but by living the life of a son in union with all mankind: "The glory of God is man fully alive" (Irenaeus).

The separate strands of consideration thus come together: the temporal and eschatological, the personal and doctrinal, the individual and communal, the intellectual and bodily, —all these find their final fusion in the Body of Christ perfected into the kingdom of God. "Because of the mediation which Christ exercises actually by his body, the happiness of heaven appears more concrete and closer to the heart of man, even though that very closeness makes the mystery of heaven deeper still."[17]

[16] Urs von Balthasar, *Science, Religion and Christianity*, p. 113.
[17] Durrwell, *Resurrection*, p. 351, n. 3.

Bibliography

BOOKS

ADAM, KARL. *The Christ of Faith*. Translated by Joyce Crick. New York, Mentor Omega Books, 1957.

AUBERT, ROGER. *Le problème de l'acte de foi*. 3rd ed. Louvain, E. Waring, 1958.

BAIERL, JOSEPH. *The Theory of Revelation*. Part I. Section I. Rochester, Seminary Press, 1927.

BAILLIE, JOHN. *The Idea of Revelation in Recent Thought*. New York, Columbia University, 1956.

BARR, JAMES. *Biblical Words for Time*. Naperville, Ill., Allenson, 1962.

BARTH, KARL. *Anselm: Fides Quaerens Intellectum*. Richmond, John Knox, 1960.

BLONDEL, MAURICE. *The Letter on Apologetics and History and Dogma*. Translated by Alexander Dru and Illtyd Trethowan. New York, Holt, Rinehart and Winston, 1964.

BOISMARD, M. E. *St. John's Prologue*. Translated by Carisbrooke Dominicans. Westminster, Newman, 1957.

BOMAN, THORLIEF. *Hebrew Thought Compared with Greek*. Translated by Jules L. Moreau. Philadelphia, Westminster, 1960.

BOROS, LADISLAUS. *The Mystery of Death*. Translated by Gregory Bainbridge. New York, Herder and Herder, 1965.

BROWN, RAYMOND. *The Sensus Plenior of Sacred Scripture*. Baltimore, St. Mary's University, 1955.

BRUNNER, EMIL. *The Christian Doctrine of God*. Translated by Olive Wyon. Philadelphia, Westminster, 1950.

189

————. *Truth as Encounter.* Translated by David Cairns. 2nd ed. Philadelphia, Westminster, 1964.

BUBER, MARTIN. *I and Thou.* Translated by Ronald Smith. New York, Scribner, 1958.

BULST, WERNER. *Revelation.* Translated by Bruce Vawter. New York, Sheed and Ward, 1965.

BULTMANN, RUDOLPH. *The Presence of Eternity.* New York, Harper and Brothers, 1957.

————. *Existence and Faith.* Translated by Schubert M. Ogden. New York, Meridian Books, 1960.

CASSERLY, J. V. LANGMEAD. *Toward a Theology of History.* London, A. R. Mowbray and Co., 1965.

CERFAUX, L. *Christ in the Theology of St. Paul.* Translated by Geoffrey Webb and Adrian Walker. New York, Herder and Herder, 1959.

CHAUCHARD, PAUL. *Science and Religion.* Translated by S. J. Tester. New York, Hawthorn Books, 1962.

CHENU, M. D. *Is Theology a Science?* Translated by A. H. N. Green-Armytage. New York, Hawthorn Books, 1959.

CIRNE-LIMA, CARLOS. *Personal Faith.* Translated by G. Richard Dimler. New York, Herder and Herder, 1965.

COLLINGWOOD, R. G. *The Idea of History.* Oxford, Clarendon Press, 1946.

CONGAR, YVES. *The Meaning of Tradition.* Translated by A. N. Woodrow. New York, Hawthorn Books, 1964.

COPPENS, J. *L'inspiration et l'inerrance bibliques.* Bruges-Paris, Desclée de Brouwer, 1957.

COX, HARVEY. *The Secular City.* New York, Macmillan, 1965.

CULLMANN, OSCAR. *Christ and Time.* Translated by Floyd Filson. Philadelphia, Westminster, 1950.

DANIÉLOU, JEAN. *Christ and Us.* Translated by Walter Roberts. New York, Sheed and Ward, 1961.

————. *The Salvation of the Nations.* Translated by Angeline Bouchard. Notre Dame, University of Notre Dame, 1962.

DE LUBAC, HENRI. *Catholicism.* Translated from 4th French edition by Lancelot Sheppard. London, Burns and Oates, 1950.

DICKIE, EDGAR PRIMROSE. *God is Light. Studies in Revelation and Personal Conviction.* New York, Charles Scribner's Sons, 1954.

DODD, C. H. *The Bible Today.* New York, Macmillan, 1947.

————. *The Apostolic Preaching and its Developments.* 3rd ed. London, Hodder and Stoughton, 1963.

190

DONDEYNE, ALBERT. *Contemporary European Thought and Christian Faith.* Translated by E. McMullen and J. Burnheim. Pittsburgh, Duquesne University, 1958.

———. *Faith and the World.* Translated by Walter van de Putte. Pittsburgh, Duquesne University, 1963.

DUROUX, BENOIT. *La psychologie de la foi chez Saint Thomas d'Aquin.* Fribourg, Angelicum, 1956.

DURRWELL, F. X. *The Resurrection.* Translated by Rosemary Sheed. New York, Sheed and Ward, 1960.

———. *In the Redeeming Christ.* Translated by Rosemary Sheed. New York, Sheed and Ward, 1963.

EICHRODT, WALTER. *Man in the Old Testament.* Translated by K. and R. Gregor Smith. London, SCM Press, 1951.

ELIADE, MIRCEA. *Cosmos and History.* Translated by Williard Trask. New York, Harper Torchbook, 1959.

FRANK, ERIC. *Philosophical Understanding and Religious Truth.* New York, Oxford, 1945.

GARDEIL, A. *La donné révélé et la théologie.* Paris, Libraire Victor Lecoffre, 1910.

GARRIGOU-LAGRANGE, REGINALD. *De Revelatione.* Vol. I. Rome, Casa Editrice Marietti, 1944.

GOGARTEN, FRIEDRICH. *Demythologizing and History.* London, SCM Press, 1955.

GOLDBRUNNER, JOSEF. *Holiness is Wholeness.* Translated by Stanley Godman, New York, Pantheon Books, 1955.

———. *Individuation.* Translated by Stanley Godman. New York, Pantheon Books, 1956.

GRANT, R. M. *The Letter and the Spirit.* New York, Macmillan, 1957.

GROSSOUW, WILLIAM. *Revelation and Redemption.* Translated by Martin Schoenberg. Westminster, Newman, 1955.

GUARDINI, ROMANO. *Die Offenbarung.* Würzburg, Werkbund Verlag, 1940.

———. *The Lord.* Translated by Elinor Castendyk Briefs. Chicago, Henry Regnery Co., 1954.

———. *The Life of Faith.* Translated by John Chapin. Westminster, Newman, 1961.

———. *The Humanity of Christ.* Translated by Ronald Walls. New York, Pantheon Books, 1964.

GUSDORF, GEORGES. *Speaking.* Translated by Paul T. Brockleman. Evanston, Northwestern University, 1965.

GUTWENGER, ENGLEBERT. *Bewusstsein und Wissen Christi.* Innsbruck, Verlag Felizian Rauch, 1960.

HEIDEGGER, MARTIN. *An Introduction to Metaphysics.* Translated by Ralph Manheim. New York, Doubleday Anchor Books, 1961.
————. *Being and Time.* Translated by John Macquarrie and Edward Robinson. London, SCM Press, 1962.

JACOB, EDMOND. *Theology of the Old Testament.* Translated by A. Heathcote and Philip Allcock. New York, Harper and Brothers, 1958.

JOLY, EUGENE. *What is Faith?* Translated by Illtyd Trethowan. New York, Hawthorn Books, 1958.

JUNGMANN, JOSEF. *The Good News Yesterday and Today.* Translated by William Huesman. New York, Sadlier, 1962.

KÜNG, HANS. *Structures of the Church.* Translated by Salvator Attanasio. New York, Thomas Nelson and Sons, 1964.

KWANT, REMY. *Encounter.* Translated by Robert C. Adolfe. Pittsburgh, Duquesne University, 1960.

LADNER, GERHART. *The Idea of Reform.* Cambridge, Harvard University, 1959.

LANG, ALBERT. *Dei Sendung Christi.* München, Max Hueber, 1957.

LATOURELLE, RENE. *Théologie de la révélation.* Bruges, Desclée de Brouwer, 1963.

LEVIE, JEAN. *The Bible, Word of God in Words of Men.* Translated by S. H. Treman. New York, P. J. Kenedy and Sons, 1961.

LEWIS, EDWIN. *The Philosophy of the Christian Revelation.* 3rd ed. London, Epworth Press, 1948.

LONERGAN, BERNARD J. F. *Insight.* New York, Longmans, Green and Co., 1957.

LÖWITH, KARL. *Meaning in History.* Chicago, Phoenix Books, 1949.

LUIJPEN, WILLIAM. *Existential Phenomenology.* Pittsburgh, Duquesne University, 1963.

MALEVEZ, LOUIS. *The Christian Message and Myth.* Translated by Olive Wyon. Westminster, Newman, 1957.

MARCEL, GABRIEL. *Men Against Humanity.* Translated by G. S. Fraser. London, Harvill Press, 1952.
————. *The Philosophy of Existentialism.* Translated by Manya Harari. New York, Citadel Press, 1962.

MARLÉ, RENÉ. *Bultmann et l'interpretation du nouveau testament.* Paris, Aubier, 1955.

McDONALD, H. D. *Theories of Revelation. An Historical Study.* London, George Allen and Unwin, 1963.

MACQUARRIE, JOHN. *Twentieth Century Religious Thought.* New York, Harper and Row, 1963.

MARÉCHAL, JOSEPH. *Le point de départ de la métaphysique.* Cahier V. Paris, Desclée de Brouwer, 1949.

MERSCH, EMILE. *Theology of the Mystical Body.* Translated by Cyril Vollert. St. Louis, B. Herder Co., 1951.

MORAN, GABRIEL. *Scripture and Tradition.* New York, Herder and Herder, 1963.

MOUROUX, JEAN. *The Christian Experience.* Translated by George Lamb. New York, Sheed and Ward, 1954.

———. *I Believe.* Translated by Michael Turner. New York, Sheed and Ward, 1959.

———. *The Mystery of Time.* Translated by John Drury. New York, Desclée, 1964.

NEBREDA, ALFONSO. *Kerygma in Crisis?* Chicago, Loyola University, 1965.

NICOLAU, MICHAEL and SALAVERRI, JOACHIM. *Sacrae Theologiae Summae.* 3rd ed. Matriti, Biblioteca de Autores Cristianos, 1955.

NIEBUHR, H. RICHARD. *The Meaning of Revelation.* New York, Macmillan, 1962.

———. *The Responsible Self.* New York, Harper and Row, 1963.

PIEPER, JOSEF. *Leisure, the Basis of Culture.* Translated by Alexander Dru. New York, Pantheon, 1952.

———. *Belief and Faith.* Translated by Richard and Clara Winston. New York, Pantheon, 1963.

RAHNER, KARL. *Schriften zur Theologie.* Band III. Einsiedeln, Benziger, 1956.

———. *Geist in Welt.* 2nd ed. München, Kösel, 1957.

———. *On the Theology of Death.* Translated by Charles Henkey. New York, Herder and Herder, 1961.

———. *Inspiration in the Bible.* Translated by Charles Henkey. New York, Herder and Herder, 1961.

———. *Theological Investigations.* Vol. I. Translated by Cornelius Ernst. Baltimore, Helicon, 1961.

———. *Theological Investigations.* Vol. II. Translated by Karl Kruger. Baltimore, Helicon, 1963.

————. *Visions and Prophecies.* Translated by Charles Henkey and Richard Strachan. London, Burns and Oates, 1963.

————. *The Christian Commitment.* Translated by Cecily Hastings. New York, Sheed and Ward, 1963.

————. *On Heresy.* Translated by W. J. O'Hara. New York: Herder and Herder, 1964.

————. *Nature and Grace.* Translated by Dinah Wharton and G. Richard Dimler. New York, Sheed and Ward, 1964.

RAHNER, KARL, and RATZINGER, JOSEF. *Offenbarung und Überlieferung.* Freiburg, Herder, 1965.

RICHARDSON, ALAN. *History Sacred and Profane.* Philadelphia, Westminster, 1964.

RICHARDSON, WILLIAM J. *Heidegger,* The Hague, Martinus Nijhoff, 1962.

ROBINSON, JAMES M. *A New Quest of the Historical Jesus.* London, SCM Press, 1959.

ROUTLEY, ERIK. *The Man for Others.* New York, Oxford University Press, 1964.

SCHILLEBEECKX, EDWARD. *Christ the Sacrament of the Encounter with God.* Translated by Paul Barrett. New York, Sheed and Ward, 1963.

————. *The Layman in the Church.* Translated by M. H. Gill and Son. New York, Alba House, 1963.

SCHMAUS, MICHAEL. *Katholische Dogmatik.* Band I. München, Hueber, 1960.

————. *Essence of Christianity.* Translated by J. Holland-Smith. Chicago, Scepter, 1961.

SEMMELROTH, OTTO. *The Preaching Word.* Translated by John Jay Hughes. New York, Herder and Herder, 1965.

TILLICH, PAUL. *Systematic Theology.* Vol. I. Chicago, University of Chicago, 1951.

————. *Dynamics of Faith.* New York, Harper Torchbook, 1957.

URS VON BALTHASAR, HANS. *Science, Religion and Christianity.* Translated by Hilda Graef. Westminster, Newman, 1958.

————. *Martin Buber and Christianity.* Translated by Alexander Dru. New York, Macmillan, 1962.

————. *A Theology of History.* New York, Sheed and Ward, 1963.

————. *Word and Revelation.* Translated by A. V. Littledale with Alexander Dru. New York, Herder and Herder, 1964.

————. *Word and Redemption.* Translated by A. V. Littledale with Alexander Dru. New York, Herder and Herder, 1965.

VAN IMSCHOOT, P. *Théologie de l'A. T.* Tournai, Desclée, 1954.

VOEGELIN, ERIC. *Order and History.* Volume I: *Israel and Revelation.* Baton Rouge, Louisiana State University, 1956.

VOLKEN, LAURENT. *Visions, Revelations and the Church.* Translated by Edward Gallagher. New York, P. J. Kenedy and Sons, 1963.

VOOGHT, PAUL DE. *Les sources de la doctrine chrétienne.* Paris, Desclée de Brouwer, 1954.

VRIEZEN, T. C. *An Outline of Old Testament Theology.* Oxford, Blackwell, 1960.

WRIGHT, G. ERNEST. *God Who Acts.* Chicago, Henry Regnery Co., 1952.

ARTICLES

ALFARO, JUAN. "Persona y gracia," in *Gregorianum,* XLI (January, 1960), pp. 5–29.

———. "Cristo glorioso, revelador del Padre," in *Christus Victor Mortis,* Rome, Gregoriana, 1958. Pp. 22–70.

———."Fides in terminologia biblica," in *Gregorianum,* XLII (1961), pp. 463–505.

———. "Une dogmatique de la révélation," in *Sciences Ecclésiastiques,* XVI (May, 1964), pp. 351–357.

ALONSO SCHÖKEL, LUIS. "Hermeneutics in the Light of Language and Literature," in *Catholic Biblical Quarterly,* XXV (1963), pp. 371–386.

BALASURIYA, S. T. "Toward a Wider Ecumenism," in *The Ecumenist,* III (January–February, 1965), pp. 23–26.

BARBOTIN, EDMOND. "Connaissance rationelle et education de la foi," in *Documentation Catechestique,* XLVI (1960), pp. 27–34.

BARR, JAMES. "Revelation through History in the Old Testament and in Modern Theology," in *New Theology No. 1,* edited by Martin E. Marty and Dean G. Peerman. New York, Macmillan, 1964. Pp. 60–74.

BAUM, GREGORY. "'Honest to God' and Traditional Theology," in *The Ecumenist,* II (May–June, 1964), pp. 65–68.

BENOIT, PIERRE. "La plénitude de sens des livres saints," in *Revue Biblique,* LXVII (1960), pp. 161–196.

———. "Révélation et inspiration," in *Revue Biblique,* LXX (1963), pp. 321–370.

195

BRINKMANN, B. "Inspiration und Kanonizität der Hl. Schrift in ihrem Verhältnis zur Kirche," in *Scholastik,* XXXIII (April, 1958), pp. 208–233.

BROWN, RAYMOND. "The *Sensus Plenior* in the Last Ten Years," in *Catholic Biblical Quarterly,* XXV (October, 1963), pp. 262–285.

————. "After Bultmann What? An Introduction to the Post-Bultmannians," in *Catholic Biblical Quarterly,* XXVI (January, 1964), pp. 1–30.

BURGHARDT, WALTER J. "Catholic Concept of Tradition in the Light of Modern Theological Thought," in *Proceedings: Sixth Annual Convention, Catholic Theological Society of America,* VI (1951), pp. 42–75.

BURRELL, DAVID. "Indwelling: Presence and Dialogue," in *Theological Studies,* XXII (March, 1961), pp. 1–17.

CAHILL, JOSEPH. "Rudolph Bultmann's Concept of Revelation," in *Catholic Biblical Quarterly,* XXIV (July, 1962), pp. 297–306.

CHARLIER, C. "Méthode historique et lecture spirituelle des Ecritures," in *Bible et vie chrétienne,* XVIII (1957), pp. 7–26.

CLARKE, THOMAS. "Some Aspects of Current Christology," in *Thought,* XXXVI (Autumn, 1961), pp. 32–43.

CONGAR, M. "Bulletin de théologie dogmatique," in *Revue des sciences philosophiques et théologiques,* XXXV (1951), pp. 591–603.

————. "Inspiration des Ecritures canoniques et apostolicité de l'Église," in *Revue des sciences philosophiques et théologiques,* XLIV (1961), pp. 32–42.

————. "Ce que Jésus a appris," in *La vie spirituelle,* CIX (December, 1963), pp. 694–706.

COOKE, BERNARD. "The Problem of Sacred Doctrine in the College," in *Modern Cathechetics,* edited by Gerard S. Sloyan. New York, Macmillan, 1963. Pp. 267–290.

————. "Theology and Catechetical Renewal," in *Pastoral Cathechetics,* edited by Johannes Hofinger and Theodore C. Stone. New York, Herder and Herder, 1964, pp. 88–104.

COPPENS, J. "Comment mieux concevoir et énoncer l'inspiration et l'inerrance des Saintes Ecritures," in *Nouvelle revue théologique,* XCVI (October, 1964), pp. 933–947.

"The Council Debate on Revelation," in *Herder Correspondence,* II (January, 1965), pp. 16–21.

CROWE, FREDERICK. "Complacency and Concern in the Thought of St.

Thomas," in *Theological Studies,* XIX (March, June, September, 1959), pp. 1–39; 198–230; 343–395.

CULLMANN, OSCAR. "Scripture and Tradition," in *Christianity Divided,* edited by Daniel Callahan, *et al.* New York, Sheed and Ward. 1961. Pp. 7–31.

DANIÉLOU, JEAN. "Parole de Dieu et mission de l'Eglise," in *Le prêtre ministre de la parole.* Paris, Union des Oeuvres Catholiques de France, 1954. Pp. 41–56.

————. Le scandale de la verité," in *Etudes,* CCCIV (January, 1960), pp. 3–17.

————. "Unité et pluralité de la pensée chrétienne," in *Etudes,* CCCXII (January, 1962), pp. 3–16.

DAVIS, CHARLES. "Theology and its Present Task," in *Theology and the University,* edited by John Coulson. Baltimore, Helicon, 1964. Pp. 107–132.

DECOURTRAY, A. "La conception johannique de la foi," in *Nouvelle revue théologique,* LXXXI (June, 1959), pp. 561–576.

DE FINANCE, JOSEPH. "Being and Subjectivity," in *Cross Currents,* VI (Spring, 1956), pp. 163–178.

DE FRAINE, L. "Revelation," in *Encyclopedic Dictionary of the Bible,* translated and adapted by Louis Hartmann from 2nd revised edition, 1954–1957. New York, McGraw-Hill, 1963, cols. 2040–2046.

DEISSLER, ALFONS. "The Fundamental Message of the Old Testament and its Proclamation Today," in *The Word. Readings in Theology,* compiled at the Canisianum. New York, P. J. Kenedy and Sons, 1963. Pp. 93–103.

DULLES, AVERY. "The Theology of Revelation," in *Theological Studies,* XXV (March, 1964), pp. 43–58.

DUMONT, C. "Unité et diversité des signes de la révélation," in *Nouvelle revue théologique,* LXXX (February, 1958), pp. 133–158.

DURAND, A. "La science du Christ," in *Nouvelle revue théologique,* LXXI (May, 1949), pp. 497–503.

EXTREMENO, P. CLAUDIO GARCIA. "El sentido de la fe, criterio de la tradicion," in *La ciencia tomista,* LXXXVII (July, 1960), pp. 569–606.

GALOT, JEAN. "Science et conscience de Jésus," in *Nouvelle revue théologique,* LXXXII (February, 1960), pp. 113–131.

GRASSO, DOMENICO. "The Good News and the Renewal of Theology," in Josef Jungmann, *The Good News Yesterday and Today,* translated by William Huesman. New York, Sadlier, 1962, pp. 201–211.

GRILLMEIER, A. "The Figure of Christ in Catholic Theology Today," in *Theology Today.* Volume I: *Renewal in Dogma,* translated by Peter White and Raymond Kelly. Milwaukee, Bruce, 1965. Pp. 66–108.

HARMON, JOHN. "Toward a Theology of the City Church," in *Cross Currents,* XIV (Autumn, 1964), pp. 401–415.

HORTON, WALTER M. "Revelation," in *Handbook of Christian Theology,* edited by M. Halverson. New York, Meridian Books, 1958. P. 327.

IUNG, N. "Révélation." *Dictionnaire de théologie catholique.* Tome XIII. Paris, Librairie letouzey et ané, 1936. Cols. 2579–2618.

JERPHAGNON, LUCIEN. "Le corps et la communication des consciences," in *L'homme au regard de la foi.* Paris, Les Editions Ouvrières, 1959. Pp. 183–193.

JOHANN, ROBERT. "Experience and Philosophy," in *Experience, Existence and the Good,* edited by Irwin C. Lieb. Carbondale, Ill., Southern Illinois University, 1961. Pp. 25–38.

JUNGMANN, JOSEF. "Theology and Kerygmatic Teaching," in *Lumen Vitae,* V (April, 1950), pp. 258–263.

KÜNG, HANS. "Justification and Sanctification According to the New Testament," in *Christianity Divided,* edited by Daniel Callahan *et al.* New York, Sheed and Ward, 1961. Pp. 309–335.

———. "Freedom and Theology," in *Social Digest,* VIII (January, 1965), pp. 4–11.

LÉONARD, A. "La foi, principe fondamental du developpement du dogme," in *Revue des sciences philosophiques et théologiques,* XLII (April, 1958), pp. 276–286.

———. "Toward a Theology of the Word of God," in *The Word. Readings in Theology,* compiled at the Canisianum. New York, P. J. Kenedy and Sons, 1964. Pp. 64–89.

LEVIE, JEAN. "Le message de Jésus dans la pensée des apôtres," in *Nouvelle revue théologique,* LXXXIII (January, 1961), pp. 25–49.

LIÉGÉ, P. A. "Contenu et pédagogie de la prédication chrétienne," in *La Maison-Dieu,* 39 (1954), pp. 23–37.

LOHFINK, N. "Über die Irrtumslösigkeit und die Einheit der Schrift," in *Stimmen der Zeit,* CLXXIV (1964), pp. 161–181.

LONERGAN, BERNARD. "Theology and Understanding," in *Gregorianum,* XXXV (1954), pp. 630–648.

————. "Christ as Subject: A Reply," in *Gregorianum*, XL (1959), pp. 242–270.

————. "Cognitional Structure," in *Continuum*, II (Autumn, 1964), pp. 530–542.

LYONNET, S. "La valeur soteriologique de la resurrection du Christ selon saint Paul," in *Christus Victor Mortis*. Rome, Gregoriana, 1958. Pp. 95–118.

MALEVEZ, LOUIS. "The Believer and the Philosopher," in *Philosophy Today*, V (Spring, 1961), pp. 14–30.

MARC, A. "L'idée de révélation," in *Gregorianum*, XXXIV (1953), pp. 390–420.

MARROU, H. I. "From the Logic of History to an Ethic for the Historian," in *Cross Currents*, XI (Winter, 1961), pp. 61–77.

McCARTHY, DENNIS. "Personality, Society and Inspiration," in *Theological Studies*, XXIV (December, 1963), pp. 553–576.

McKENZIE, JOHN L. "Problems of Hermeneutics in Roman Catholic Exegesis," in *Journal of Biblical Studies*, LXXVII (1958), pp. 197–204.

————. "The Word of God in the Old Testament," in *Theological Studies*, XXI (June, 1960), pp. 183–206.

————. "The Social Character of Inspiration," in *Catholic Biblical Quarterly*, XXIV (April, 1962), pp. 115–24.

MOELLER, CHARLES. "Is It Possible, in the Twentieth Century, to be a Man of the Bible?" in *Liturgy and the Word of God*. Collegeville, Liturgical Press, 1959. Pp. 119–156.

MORAN, GABRIEL. "Faith as Aim in Religious Education," in *Catholic Educational Review*, LXI (February, 1963), pp. 113–121.

————. "Hope: Foundation of Religious Education," in *Catholic Educational Review*, LXI (May, 1963), pp. 302–312.

————. "Scripture-Tradition: Witness to Revelation," in *Continuum*, I (Autumn, 1963), pp. 343–354.

————. "What is Revelation?" in *Theological Studies*, XXV (June, 1964), pp. 217–231.

————. "Freedom in Christian Revelation," in *Proceedings: Eleventh Annual Convention of The Society of Catholic College Teachers of Sacred Doctrine*, XI (1965), pp. 59–79.

NEBREDA, ALFONSO. "The Preparation of the Message," in *Faith and Commitment*, edited by Mark Link. Chicago, Loyola, 1964. Pp. 186–203.

———. "Role of Witness in Transmitting the Message," in *Pastoral Catechetics,* edited by Johannes Hofinger and Theodore C. Stone. New York, Herder and Herder, 1964. Pp. 67–86.

NICOLAS, J. H. "La foi et les signes," in *Supplément de la vie spirituelle,* XXV (May, 1953), pp. 121–164.

OEPKE, ALBRECHT. "Offenbarung," in *Theologisches Wörterbuch zum Neuen Testament.* Band III. Stuttgart, W. Kohlmammer, 1938. Pp. 565–597.

RAHNER, KARL. "Reflexions théologiques sur l'Incarnation," in *Sciences Ecclésiastiques,* XII (1960), pp. 5–19.

———. "Christianity and Non-Christian Religions," in *The Church. Readings in Theology,* compiled at the Canisianum. New York, P. J. Kenedy and Sons, 1963. Pp. 112–135.

———. "Priest and Poet," in *The Word. Readings in Theology,* compiled at the Canisianum. New York, P. J. Kenedy and Sons, 1964. Pp. 3–26.

———. "Dogmatic Considerations on Knowledge and Consciousness in Christ," in *Dogmatic vs. Biblical Theology,* edited by Herbert Vorgrimler. Baltimore, Helicon, 1964. Pp. 241–267.

RICHARDSON, CYRIL. "Word and Sacrament in Protestant Worship," in *Ecumenical Dialogue at Harvard,* edited by Samuel Miller and G. Ernest Wright. Cambridge, Harvard University, 1964. Pp. 152–171.

ROBINSON, JAMES M. "Scripture and Theological Method," in *Catholic Biblical Quarterly,* XXVII (January, 1965), pp. 6–27.

ROMERO, ANDRÉS A. ESTEBAN. "La controversia en torno a la teología kerigmática," in *XV Semana Española de Teología.* Madrid, 1956, pp. 369–409.

"La schéma sur la Révélation," in *La documentation catholique,* November 1, 1964. Cols. 1393–1422.

SCHILLEBEECKX, EDWARD. "Parole et sacrement dans l'Eglise," *Lumière et vie.* IX (January, 1960), pp. 25–45.

———. "The Church and Mankind," in *The Church and Mankind,* edited by Karl Rahner and Edward Schillebeeckx. New York, Paulist Press, 1965. Pp. 69–102.

———. "Exegesis, Dogmatics and the Development of Dogma," in *Dogmatic vs. Biblical Theology,* edited by Herbert Vorgrimler. Baltimore, Helicon, 1964. Pp. 115–145.

SCHNACKENBURG, RUDOLF. "Zum Offenbarungsgedanken in der Bibel," in *Biblische Zeitschrift,* VII (January, 1963), pp. 2–22.

————. "The Dogmatic Evaluation of the New Testament," in *Dogmatic vs. Biblical Theology,* edited by Herbert Vorgrimler. Baltimore, Helicon, 1964. Pp. 147–172.

SIMON, J. M. "La Révélation et l'Eglise," in *Revue de l'Université d'Ottawa,* XXXIV (January, 1964), pp. 38*–61*.

STANLEY, DAVID. "The Conception of Our Gospels as Salvation History," in *Theological Studies,* XX (December, 1959), pp. 561–589.

STUHLMUELLER, CARROLL. "The Influence of Oral Tradition upon Exegesis," in *Catholic Biblical Quarterly,* XX (July, 1958), pp. 299–326.

TAVARD, GEORGE. "Scripture and Tradition: Source or Sources," in *Journal of Ecumenical Studies,* I (Autumn, 1964), pp. 445–459.

THORNHILL, JOHN. "Toward an Integral Theology," in *Theological Studies,* XXIV (June, 1963), pp. 264–277.

URS VON BALTHASAR, HANS. "God Speaks as Man," in *Word and Revelation,* translated by A. V. Littledale with Alexander Dru. New York, Herder and Herder, 1964. Pp. 87–119.

————. "The Freedom of the Subject," in *Cross Currents,* XII (Winter, 1962), pp. 13–30.

VAWTER, BRUCE. "The Historical Theology of the Gospels," in *Homiletic and Pastoral Review,* LXII (May, 1962), pp. 681–691.

————. "The Fuller Sense: Some Considerations," *Catholic Biblical Quarterly,* XXVI (January, 1964), pp. 85–96.

VIELMO, C. G. "De Verbi Dei revelatione et Spiritus Dei communicatione," *Divus Thomas,* LXVII (January, 1964), pp. 3–21.

WEIGEL, G. "The Meaning of Sacred Doctrine in the College," in *Shaping the Christian Message,* edited by Gerard S. Sloyan. New York, Macmillan, 1958. Pp. 170–182.

WHITE, VICTOR. "St. Thomas's Conception of Revelation," *Dominican Studies,* I (January, 1948), pp. 3–34.

Appendix

Constitution on Divine Revelation

PREFACE

1. Hearing the word of God with reverence and proclaiming it with faith, the sacred synod takes its direction from these words of St. John: "We announce to you the eternal life which dwelt with the Father and was made visible to us. What we have seen and heard we announce to you, so that you may have fellowship with us and our common fellowship be with the Father and His Son Jesus Christ" (1 Jn. 1:2–3. Therefore, following in the footsteps of the Council of Trent and of the First Vatican Council, this present council wishes to set forth authentic doctrine on divine revelation and how it is handed on, so that by hearing the message of salvation the whole world may believe, by believing it may hope, and by hoping it may love.[1]

CHAPTER I
REVELATION ITSELF

2. In his goodness and wisdom God chose to reveal himself and to make known to us the hidden purpose of his will (see Eph. 1:9) by which through Christ, the Word made flesh, man might in the Holy Spirit have access to the Father and come to share in the divine nature (see Eph. 2:18; 2 Pet. 1:4). Through this revelation, therefore, the invisible God (see Col. 1:15, 1 Tim. 1:17) out of the abundance of his love speaks to men as friends (see Ex. 33:11; Jn. 15:14–15) and lives among them (see Bar. 3:38), so that he may invite and take them into fellowship with himself. This plan of revelation is realized by deeds and words having an inner unity: the deeds wrought by God in the history of salvation manifest and con-

[1] See St. Augustine, "De Catechizandis Rudibus," c. IV, 8: *PL* 40, 316.

202

firm the teaching and realities signified by the words, while the words proclaim the deeds and clarify the mystery contained in them. By this revelation then, the deepest truth about God and the salvation of man shines out for our sake in Christ, who is both the mediator and the fullness of all revelation.[2]

3. God, who through the Word creates all things (see Jn. 1:3) and keeps them in existence, gives men an enduring witness to Himself in created realities (see Rom. 1:19–20). Planning to make known the way of heavenly salvation, He went further and from the start manifested himself to our first parents. Then after their fall his promise of redemption aroused in them the hope of being saved (see Gen. 3:15) and from that time on he ceaselessly kept the human race in his care, to give eternal life to those who perseveringly do good in search of salvation (see Rom. 2:6–7). Then, at the time He had appointed he called Abraham in order to make of him a great nation (see Gen. 12:2). Through the patriarchs, and after them through Moses and the prophets, he taught this people to acknowledge himself the one living and true God, provident father and just judge, and to wait for the Saviour promised by him, and in this manner prepared the way for the Gospel down through the centuries.

4. Then, after speaking in many and varied ways through the prophets, "now at last in these days God has spoken to us in his Son" (Heb. 1:1–2). For he sent his Son, the eternal Word, who enlightens all men, so that he might dwell among men and tell them of the innermost being of God (see Jn. 1:1–18). Jesus Christ, therefore, the Word made flesh, was sent as "a man to men."[3] He "speaks the words of God" (Jn. 3:34), and completes the work of salvation which his Father gave him to do (see Jn. 5:36, 17:4). To see Jesus is to see his Father (Jn. 14:9). For this reason Jesus perfected revelation by fulfilling it through his whole work of making himself present and manifesting himself: through his words and deeds, his signs and wonders, but especially through his death and glorious resurrection from the dead and final sending of the Spirit of truth. Moreover, he confirmed with divine testimony what revelation proclaimed, that God is with us to free us from the darkness of sin and death, and to raise us up to life eternal.

[2] Cf. Mt. 11:27; Jn. 1:14 and 17; 14:6; 17:1–3; 2 Cor. 3:16 and 4:6; Eph. 1:3–14.

[3] "Epistle to Diognetus," c. VII, 4.

The Christian dispensation, therefore, as the new and definitive covenant, will never pass away, and we now await no further new public revelation before the glorious manifestation of our Lord Jesus Christ (see 1 Tim. 6:14 and Tit. 2:13).

5. "The obedience of faith" (Rom. 13:26; see 1:5; 2 Cor. 10:5–6) "is to be given to God who reveals, an obedience by which man commits his whole self freely to God, offering the full submission of intellect and will to God who reveals,"[4] and freely assenting to the truth revealed by him. To make this act of faith, the grace of God and the interior help of the Holy Spirit must precede and assist, moving the heart and turning it to God, opening the eyes of the mind and giving "joy and ease to everyone in assenting to the truth and believing it."[5] To bring about an ever deeper understanding of revelation the same Holy Spirit constantly brings faith to completion by his gifts.

6. Through divine revelation, God chose to show forth and communicate himself and the eternal decisions of his will regarding the salvation of men. That is to say, he chose to share with them those divine treasures which totally transcend the understanding of the human mind.[6]

As a sacred synod has affirmed, God, the beginning and end of all things, can be known with certainty from created reality by the light of human reason (see Rom. 1:20); but it teaches that it is "through his revelation that those religious truths which are by their nature accessible to human reason can be known by all men with ease, with solid certitude and with no trace of error, even in this present state of the human race."[7]

CHAPTER II
HANDING ON DIVINE REVELATION

7. In his gracious goodness, God has seen to it that what he had revealed for the salvation of all nations would abide perpetually in its full integrity and be handed on to all generations. Therefore

[4] First Vatican Council, *Dogmatic Constitution on the Catholic Faith*, Chapter 3, "On Faith": *Denzinger* 1789 (3008).

[5] Second Council of Orange, Canon 7: *Denz.* 180 (377); First Vatican Council, *loc. cit.: Denz.* 1791 (3010).

[6] First Vatican Council, *Dogmatic Constitution on the Catholic Faith*, Chapter 2, "On Revelation": *Denz.* 1786 (3005).

[7] *Ibid: Denz.* 1785 and 1786 (3004 and 3005).

Christ the Lord in whom the full revelation of the supreme God is brought to completion (see Cor. 1:20; 3:13; 4:6), commissioned the apostles to preach to all men that Gospel which is the source of all saving truth and moral teaching,[1] and to impart to them heavenly gifts. This Gospel had been promised in former times through the prophets, and Christ himself had fulfilled it and promulgated it with his lips. This commission was faithfully fulfilled by the apostles who, by their oral preaching, by example, and by observances, handed on what they had received from the lips of Christ, from living with him, and from what he did, or what they had learned through the prompting of the Holy Spirit. The commission was fulfilled, too, by those apostles and apostolic men who under the inspiration of the same Holy Spirit committed the message of salvation to writing.[2]

But in order to keep the Gospel forever whole and alive within the Church, the apostles left bishops as their successors, "handing on" to them "the authority to teach in their own place."[3] This sacred tradition, therefore, and sacred Scripture of both the Old and New Testaments are like a mirror in which the pilgrim Church on earth looks at God, from whom she has received everything, until she is brought finally to see him, face to face, as he is (see 1 Jn. 3:2).

8. And so the apostolic preaching, which is expressed in a special way in the inspired books, was to be preserved by an unending succession of preachers until the end of time. Therefore, the apostles, handing on what they themselves had received, warn the faithful to hold fast to the traditions which they have learned either by word of mouth or by letter (see 2 Thess. 2:15), and to fight in defense of the faith handed on once and for all (see Jud. 3).[4] Now what was handed on by the apostles includes everything which contributes towards the holiness of life and increase in faith of the people of God; and so the Church, in her teaching, life, and worship, perpetuates and hands on to all generations all that she herself is, all that she believes.

[1] See Mt. 28:19–20, and Mk. 16:15; Council of Trent, Session IV. *Decree on Scriptural Canons: Denz.* 783 (1501).

[2] See Council of Trent, *loc. cit.;* First Vatican Council, Session III, *Dogmatic Constitution on the Catholic Faith,* Chapter 2, "On Revelation": *Denz.* 1787 (3006).

[3] St. Irenaeus, "Against Heretics," III, 3, 1: *PG* 7, 848.

[4] See Second Council of Nicaea: Denzinger 303 (602); Fourth Council of Constance, Session X, Canon 1: *Denz.* 336 (650–652).

This tradition which comes from the apostles develops in the Church with the help of the Holy Spirit.[5] For there is a growth in the understanding of the realities and the words which have been handed down. This happens through the contemplation and study made by believers, who treasure these things in their hearts (see Lk. 2:19, 51) through a penetrating understanding of the spiritual realities which they experience, and through the preaching of those who have received through episcopal succession the sure gift of truth. For as the centuries succeed one another, the Church constantly moves forward toward the fullness of divine truth until the words of God reach their complete fulfillment in her.

The words of the holy fathers witness to the presence of this living tradition, whose wealth is poured into the practice and life of the believing and praying Church. Through the same tradition the Church's full canon of the sacred books is known, and the sacred writings themselves are more profoundly understood and unceasingly made active in her; and thus God, who spoke of old, uninterruptedly converses with the bride of his beloved Son; and the Holy Spirit, through whom the living voice of the Gospel resounds in the Church, and through her, in the world, leads unto all truth those who believe and makes the word of Christ dwell abundantly in them (see Col. 3:16).

9. Hence there exists a close connection and communication between sacred tradition and sacred Scripture. For both of them, flowing from the same divine wellspring, in a certain way merge into a unity and tend towards the same end. For sacred Scripture is the word of God inasmuch as it is consigned to writing under the inspiration of the divine Spirit, while sacred tradition takes the word of God entrusted by Christ the Lord and the Holy Spirit to the apostles, and hands it on to their successors in its full purity, so that led by the light of the Spirit of truth, they may in proclaiming it preserve this word of God faithfully, explain it, and make it more widely known. Consequently, it is not from sacred Scripture alone that the Church draws her certainty about everything which has been revealed. Therefore, both sacred tradition and sacred Scripture are to be accepted and venerated with the same sense of devotion and reverence.[6]

[5] See First Vatican Council, *Dogmatic Constitution on the Catholic Faith,* Chapter 4, "On Faith and Reason": *Denz.* 1800 (3020).
[6] See Council of Trent, Session IV, *loc. cit.: Denz.* 783 (1501).

10. Sacred tradition and sacred Scripture form one sacred deposit of the word of God, committed to the Church. Holding fast to this deposit the entire holy people united with their shepherds remain always steadfast in the teaching of the Apostles, in the common life, in the breaking of the bread, and in prayers (see Acts 2:42, Greek text), so that holding to, practicing, and professing the heritage of the faith, it becomes on the part of the bishops and faithful a single common effort.[7]

But the task of authentically interpreting the word of God, whether written or handed on,[8] has been entrusted exclusively to the living teaching office of the Church,[9] whose authority is exercised in the name of Jesus Christ. This teaching office is not above the word of God, but serves it, teaching only what has been handed on, listening to it devoutly, guarding it scrupulously, and explaining it faithfully in accord with a divine commission and with the help of the Holy Spirit; it draws from this one deposit of faith everything which it presents for belief as divinely revealed.

It is clear, therefore, that sacred tradition, sacred Scripture and the teaching authority of the Church, in accord with God's most wise design, are so linked and joined together that one cannot stand without the others, and that all together and each in its own way under the action of the one Holy Spirit contribute effectively to the salvation of souls.

CHAPTER III
SACRED SCRIPTURE, ITS INSPIRATION,
AND DIVINE INTERPRETATION

11. Those divinely revealed realities which are contained and presented in sacred Scripture have been committed to writing under the inspiration of the Holy Spirit. For holy mother Church, relying on the belief of the apostles (see Jn. 20:31; 2 Tim. 3:16; 2 Pet. 1:19–20,

[7] See Pius XII, apostolic constitution *Munificentissimus Deus*, November 1, 1950: *AAS*, 42 (1950), p. 756; *Collected Writings of St. Cyprian*, "Letter 66, 8." "The Church [is] people united with the priest and the pastor together with his flock."

[8] See First Vatican Council, *Dogmatic Constitution on the Catholic Faith*, Chapter 3, "On Faith": *Denz.* 1792 (3011).

[9] See Pius XII, encyclical *Humani generis*, August 12, 1950: *AAS*, 42 (1950), pp. 568–569: *Denz.* 2314 (3886).

3:15–16), holds that the books of both the Old and New Testaments in their entirety, with all their parts, are sacred and canonical because written under the inspiration of the Holy Spirit, they have God as their author and have been handed on as such to the Church herself.[1] In composing the sacred books, God chose men, and while employed by him[2] they made use of their powers and abilities, so that with him acting in them and through them,[3] they, as true authors, consigned to writing everything and only those things which he wanted.[4]

Therefore, since everything asserted by the inspired authors or sacred writers must be held to be asserted by the Holy Spirit, it follows that the books of Scripture must be acknowledged as teaching solidly, faithfully, and without error that truth which God wanted put into the sacred writings[5] for the sake of our salvation. Therefore, "all Scripture is divinely inspired and has its use for teaching the truth and refuting error, for reformation of manners and discipline in right living, so that the man who belongs to God may be efficient and equipped for good work of every kind" (2 Tim. 3:16–17, Greek text).

12. However, since God speaks in sacred Scripture through men in human fashion,[6] the interpreter of sacred Scripture, in order to see clearly what God wanted to communicate to us, should carefully investigate what meaning the sacred writers really intended, and what God wanted to manifest by means of their words.

[1] See First Vatican Council, *Dogmatic Constitution on the Catholic Faith,* Chapter 2, "On Revelation": *Denz.* 1787 (3006); Biblical Commission, decree of June 18, 1915: *Denz.* 2180 (3629): *Enchiridion Biblicum* 420; Holy Office, epistle of December 22, 1923: *EB* 499.

[2] See Pius XII, encyclical *Divino afflante Spiritu,* September 30, 1943: *AAS,* 35 (1943), p. 314; *EB* 556.

[3] "In" and "for" man: see Heb. 1, and 4:7; ("in"): 2. Sm. 23:2; Mt. 1:22 and various places; ("for"): First Vatican Council, *Schema on Catholic Doctrine,* note 9: *Coll. Lac.,* VII, 522.

[4] Leo XIII, encyclical *Providentissimus Deus,* November 18, 1893: *Denz.* 1952 (3293); *EB* 125.

[5] See St. Augustine, "Gen. ad Litt.," 2, 9, 20: *PL* 34, 270–271; "Epistle," 82, 3: *PL* 33, 277: *Corpus Scriptorum Ecclesasticorum Latinorum* 34, 2, p. 354.

St. Thomas, *On Truth,* q. 12, a. 2, c.

Council of Trent, Session IV, Scriptural Canons: *Denz.* 783 (1501).

Leo XIII, encyclical *Providentissimus Deus: EB* 121, 124, 126–127.

Pius XII, encyclical *Divino afflante Spiritu: EB* 539.

[6] St. Augustine, "City of God," XVII, 6, 2: *PL* 41,537; *CSEL* XL, 2,228.

To search out the intention of the sacred writers, attention should be given, among other things, to "literary forms." For truth is set forth and expressed differently in texts which are variously historical, prophetic, poetic, or of other forms of discourse. The interpreter must investigate what meaning the sacred writer intended to express and actually expressed in particular circumstances by using contemporary literary forms in accordance with the situation of his own time and culture.[7] For the correct understanding of what the sacred author wanted to assert, due attention must be paid to the customary and characteristic styles of feeling, speaking, and narrating which prevailed at the time of the sacred writer, and to the patterns men normally employed at that period in their everyday dealings with one another.[8]

But, since sacred Scripture must be read and interpreted in the same spirit in which it was written,[9] no less serious attention must be given to the content and unity of the whole of Scripture if the meaning of the sacred texts is to be correctly worked out. The living tradition of the whole Church must be taken into account along with the harmony which exists between elements of the faith. It is the task of exegetes to work according to these rules towards a better understanding and explanation of the meaning of sacred Scripture, so that through preparatory study the judgment of the Church may mature. For all of what has been said about the way of interpreting Scripture is subject finally to the judgment of the Church, which carries out the divine commisison and ministry of guarding and interpreting the word of God.[10]

13. In sacred Scripture, therefore, while the truth and holiness of God always remains intact, the marvelous "condescension" of eternal wisdom is clearly shown, "that we may learn the gentle kindness of God, which words cannot express, and how far he has gone in adapting his language with thoughtful concern for our weak human nature."[11] For the words of God, expressed in human language, have been made

---

[7] St. Augustine, "On Christian Doctrine," III, 18, 26; *PL* 34, 75–76.

[8] Pius XII, *loc. cit.: Denz.* 2294 (3829–3930); *EB* 557–562.

[9] See Benedict XV, encyclical *Spiritus Paraclitus,* September 15, 1920: *EB* 469. St. Jerome, "In Galatians," 5, 19–20: *PL* 26, 417A.

[10] See First Vatican Council, *Dogmatic Constitution on the Catholic Faith,* Chapter 2, "On Revelation": *Denz.* 1788 (3007).

[11] St. John Chrysostom, "In Genesis" 3, 8 (Homily 17, 1): *PG* 53, 134; *"attemperatio"* [in English "suitable adjustment"] is translated into Greek by *"synkatabasis."*

like human discourse, just as the word of the eternal Father, when he took to himself the flesh of human weakness, was in every way made like men.

CHAPTER IV
THE OLD TESTAMENT

14. In carefully planning and preparing the salvation of the whole human race the God of infinite love, by a special dispensation, chose for himself a people to whom he would entrust his promises. First he entered into a covenant with Abraham (see Gen. 15:18) and, through Moses, with the people of Israel (see Ex. 24:8). To this people which he had acquired for himself, he so manifested himself through words and deeds as the one true and living God that Israel came to know by experience the ways of God with men. Then, too, when God himself spoke to them through the mouth of the prophets, Israel daily gained a deeper and clearer understanding of his ways and made them more widely known among the nations (see Pss. 21:29, 95:1–3; Is. 2:1–5; Jer. 3:17). The plan of salvation foretold by the sacred authors, recounted and explained by them, is found as the true word of God in the books of the Old Testament: these books, therefore, written under divine inspiration, remain permanently valuable. "For all that was written for our instruction, so that by steadfastness and the encouragement of the Scriptures we might have hope" (Rom. 15:4).

15. The principal purpose to which the plan of the Old Covenant was directed was to prepare for the coming of Christ, the redeemer of all and of the messianic kingdom, to announce this coming by prophecy (see Lk. 24:44; Jn. 5:39; 1 Pet. 1:10), and to indicate its meaning through various types (see 1 Cor. 10:12). Now the books of the Old Testament, in accordance with the state of mankind before the time of salvation established by Christ, reveal to all men the knowledge of God and of man and the ways in which God, just and merciful, deals with men. These books, though they also contain some things which are incomplete and temporary, nevertheless show us true divine pedagogy.[1] These same books, then, give expression to a lively sense of God, contain a store of sublime teachings about God, sound wisdom about human life, and a wonderful treasury of prayers, and in them the

[1] Pius XI, encyclical *Mit Brennender Sorge*, March 14, 1937: *AAS*, 29 (1937), p. 51.

mystery of our salvation is present in a hidden way. Christians should receive them with reverence.

16. God, the inspirer and author of both Testaments, wisely arranged that the New Testament be hidden in the Old and the Old be made manifest in the new.[2] For, though Christ established the New Covenant in his blood (see Lk. 22:20; 1 Cor. 11:25), still the books of the Old Testament with all their parts, caught up into the proclamation of the Gospel,[3] acquire and show forth their full meaning in the New Testament (see Mat. 5:17; Lk. 24:27; Rom. 16:25–26; 2 Cor. 14:16) and in turn shed light on it and explain it.

CHAPTER V
THE NEW TESTAMENT

17. The word of God, which is the power of God for the salvation of all who believe (see Rom. 1:16), is set forth and shows its power in a most excellent way in the writings of the New Testament. For when the fullness of time arrived (see Gal. 4:4), the Word was made flesh and dwelt among us in his fullness of grace and truth (see Jn. 1:14). Christ established the kingdom of God on earth, manifested his Father and himself by deeds and words, and completed his work by his death, resurrection, and glorious ascension and by the sending of the Holy Spirit. Having been lifted up from the earth, he draws all men to himself (see Jn. 12:32, Greek text), he who alone has the words of eternal life (see Jn. 6:68). This mystery had not been manifested to other generations as it was now revealed to his holy apostles and prophets in the Holy Spirit (see Eph. 3:4–6, Greek text), so that they might preach the Gospel, stir up faith in Jesus, Christ and Lord, and gather together the Church. Now the writings of the New Testament stand as a perpetual and divine witness to these realities.

18. It is common knowledge that among all the Scriptures, even those of the New Testament, the Gospels have a special preeminence, and rightly so, for they are the principal witness for the life and teaching of the incarnate Word, our Saviour.

The Church has always and everywhere held and continues to hold

[2] St. Augustine, "Quest. in Hept.," 2, 73: *PL* 34, 623.

[3] St. Irenaeus, "Against Heretics," III, 21, 3: *PG* 7, 950 (same as 25, 1: Harvey 2, p. 115). St. Cyril of Jerusalem, "Catech.," 4, 35; *PG* 33, 497. Theodore of Mopsuestia, "In Soph.," 1, 4–6: *PG* 66, 452D–453A.

that the four Gospels are of apostolic origin. For what the apostles preached in fulfillment of the commission of Christ, afterwards they themselves and apostolic men, under the inspiration of the divine Spirit, handed on to us in writing: the foundation of faith, namely, the four-fold Gospel, according to Matthew, Mark, Luke, and John.[1]

19. Holy Mother Church has firmly and with absolute constancy held, and continues to hold, that the four Gospels just named, whose historical character the Church unhesitatingly asserts, faithfully hand on what Jesus Christ, while living among men, really did and taught for their eternal salvation until the day he was taken up into heaven (see Acts 1:1). After the ascension of the Lord, instructed by the glorious events of Christ's life and taught by the light of the Spirit of truth,[2] the apostles with the clearer understanding which they then enjoyed handed on to their hearers what he had said and done.[3] The sacred authors wrote the four Gospels, selecting some things from the many which had been handed on by word of mouth or in writing, reducing some of them to a synthesis, explaining some things in view of the situation of their churches, and preserving the form of proclamation but always in such fashion that they told us the honest truth about Jesus[4]. For their intention in writing was that either from their own memory and recollections, or from the witness of those who "themselves from the beginning were eyewitnesses and ministers of the Word," we might know "the truth" concerning those matters about which we have been instructed (see Lk. 1:2–4).

20. Besides the four Gospels, the canon of the New Testament also contains the epistles of St. Paul and other apostolic writings, composed under the inspiration of the Holy Spirit, by which, according to the wise plan of God, those matters which concern Christ the Lord are confirmed, his true teaching is more and more fully stated, the saving power of the divine work of Christ is preached, the story is told of the beginnings of the Church and its marvelous growth, and its glorious fulfillment is foretold.

For the Lord Jesus was with his apostles as he had promised (see

[1] See St. Irenaeus, "Against Heretics," III, 11, 8: *PG* 7, 885.
[2] See Jn. 14:26; 16:13.
[3] Jn. 2:22; 12:16; see 14:26; 16:12–13; 7:39.
[4] See instruction "Holy Mother Church," edited by Pontifical Consilium for Promotion of Bible Studies: *AAS*, 56 (1964), p. 715.

212

Mt. 28:20) and sent them the advocate Spirit who would lead them into the fullness of truth (see Jn. 16:13).

CHAPTER VI
SACRED SCRIPTURE IN THE LIFE OF THE CHURCH

21. The Church has always venerated the divine Scriptures just as she venerates the body of the Lord, since, especially in the sacred liturgy, she unceasingly receives and offers to the faithful the bread of life from the table both of God's word and of Christ's body. She has always maintained them, and continues to do so, together with sacred tradition, as the supreme rule of faith, since, as inspired by God and committed once and for all to writing, they impart the word of God himself without change, and make the voice of the Holy Spirit resound in the words of the prophets and apostles. Therefore, like the Christian religion itself, all the preaching of the Church must be nourished and regulated by sacred Scripture. For in the sacred books, the Father who is in heaven meets his children with great love and speaks with them; and the force and power in the word of God is so great that it stands as the support and energy of the Church, the strength of faith for her sons, the food of the soul, the pure and everlasting source of spiritual life. Consequently, these words are perfectly applicable to sacred Scripture: "For the word of God is living and active" (Heb. 4:12) and "it has power to build you up and give you your heritage among all those who are sanctified" (Acts 20:32; see 1 Thess. 2:13).

22. Easy access to sacred Scripture should be provided for all the Christian faithful. That is why the Church from the very beginning accepted as her own that very ancient Greek translation of the Old Testament which is called the Septuagint; and she has always given a place of honor to other Eastern translations and Latin ones, especially the Latin translation known as the Vulgate. But since the word of God should be accessible at all times, the Church by her authority and with maternal concern sees to it that suitable and correct translations are made into different languages, especially from the original texts of the sacred books. And should the opportunity arise and the Church authorities approve, if these translations are produced in cooperation with the separated brethren as well, all Christians will be able to use them.

23. The bride of the incarnate Word, the Church taught by the Holy Spirit, is concerned to move ahead towards a deeper understanding of the sacred Scriptures so that she may increasingly feed her sons with

213

the divine words. Therefore, she also encourages the study of the holy fathers of both East and West and of sacred liturgies. Catholic exegetes then and other students of sacred theology, working diligently together and using appropriate means, should devote their energies, under the watchful care of the sacred teaching office of the Church, to an exploration and exposition of the divine writings. This should be so done that as many ministers of the divine word as possible will be able effectively to provide the nourishment of the Scriptures for the people of God, to enlighten their minds, strengthen their wills, and set men's hearts on fire with the love of God.[1] The sacred synod encourages the sons of the Church and biblical scholars to continue energetically, following the mind of the Church, with the work they have so well begun, with a constant renewal of vigor.[2]

24. Sacred theology rests on the written word of God, together with sacred tradition, as its primary and perpetual foundation. By scrutinizing in the light of faith all truth stored up in the mystery of Christ, theology is most powerfully strengthened and constantly rejuvenated by that word. For the sacred Scriptures contain the word of God and since they are inspired really are the word of God; and so the study of the sacred page is, as it were, the soul of sacred theology.[3] By the same word of Scripture the ministry of the word also, that is, pastoral preaching, catechetics, and all Christian instruction, in which the liturgical homily must hold the foremost place, is nourished in a healthy way and flourishes in a holy way.

25. Therefore, all the clergy must hold fast to the sacred Scriptures through diligent sacred reading and careful study, especially the priests of Christ and others, such as deacons and catechists who are legitimately active in the ministry of the word. This is to be done so that none of them will become "an empty preacher of the word of God outwardly, who is not a listener to it inwardly,"[4] since they must share the abundant wealth of the divine word with the faithful committed to them, especially in the sacred liturgy. The sacred synod also earnestly and especially urges all the Christian faithful, especially religious, to

[1] See Pius XII, encyclical *Divino afflante Spiritu: EB* 551, 553, 567.

Pontifical Biblical Commission, "Instruction on Proper Teaching of Sacred Scripture in Seminaries and Religious Colleges," May 13, 1950: *AAS,* 42 (1950), pp. 495–505.

[2] See Pius XII, *ibid.: EB* 569.

[3] See Leo XIII, encyclical *Providentissimus Deus: EB* 114; Benedict XV, encyclical *Spiritus Paraclitus: EB* 483.

[4] St. Augustine, "Sermons," 179, 1: *PL* 38, 966.

learn by frequent reading of the divine Scriptures the "excellent knowledge of Jesus Christ" (Phil. 3:8). "For ignorance of the Scriptures is ignorance of Christ."[5] Therefore, they should gladly put themselves in touch with the sacred text itself, whether it be through the liturgy, rich in the divine word, or through devotional reading, or through insructions suitable for the purpose and other aids which, in our time, with approval and active support of the shepherds of the Church, are commendably spread everywhere. And let them remember that prayer should accompany the reading of sacred Scripture, so that God and man may talk together; for "we speak to him when we pray; we hear him when we read the divine saying."[6]

It devolves on sacred bishops "who have the apostolic teaching"[7] to give the faithful entrusted to them suitable instruction in the right use of the divine books, especially the New Testament and above all the Gospels. This can be done through translations of the sacred texts, which are to be provided with the necessary and really adequate explanations so that the children of the Church may safely and profitably become conversant with the sacred Scriptures and be penetrated with their spirit.

Furthermore, editions of the sacred Scriptures, provided with suitable footnotes, should be prepared also for the use of non-Christians and adapted to their situation. Both pastors of souls and Christians generally should see to the wise distribution of these in one way or another.

26. In this way, therefore, through the reading and study of the sacred books, "the word of God may spread rapidly and be glorified" (2 Thess. 3:1) and the treasure of revelation, entrusted to the Church, may more and more fill the hearts of men. Just as the life of the Church is strengthened through more frequent celebration of the eucharistic mystery, similarly we may hope for a new stimulus for the life of the Spirit from a growing reverence for the word of God, which "lasts forever" (Is. 40:8; see 1 Pet. 1:23–25).

---

[5] St. Jerome, "Commentary on Isaiah, Prol.": *PL* 24, 17.
See Benedict XV, encyclical *Siritus Paraclitus: EB* 475–480; Pius XII, encyclical *Divino afflante Spiritu: EB* 544.
[6] St. Ambrose, "On the Duties of Ministers" I, 20, 88: *PL* 16, 50.
[7] St. Irenaeus, "Against Heretics" IV, 32, 1: *PG* 7, 1071.

Index

217

221

Prophet, Christ as, 60, 71; Christian as, 118; in the primitive Church, 89; Israelite, 44, 46–48
Protestantism, contemporary notions of revelation in, 35, 38, 81; doctrine and, 131; philosophy and, 33; Scripture, 95
Puech, Henri-Charles, 42 n. 8, 52 n. 27

Rahner, Karl, 34, 52 n. 26, 59 n. 3, 63 n. 15, 64, 65 n. 22, 66 n. 28, 70 n. 32, 72 n. 36, 78 n. 3, 84 n. 12, 87 n. 18 and n. 19, 89 n. 21, 98 n. 3, 101, 103 n. 15, 107 n. 23, 108 n. 24, 112 n. 33, 113 n. 35, 121, 130, 135 n. 5, 136 n. 7, 137 n. 9, 139 n. 12, 142 n. 17, 145 n. 25, 149 n. 2, 150 n. 4, 153 n. 11, 163 n. 3, 165 n. 7, 166 n. 8, 167 n. 11, 170 n. 14, 173 n. 19, 174 n. 21, 177 n. 24, 178 n. 25, 183 n. 7, 184 n. 8, 186 n. 13, 187 n. 14
Rationalism, 23, 83, 144
Ratzinger, Josef, 122 n. 13
Religious experience, 30, 151; modernism and, 29
Resurrection, 186; of Christ: see Jesus Christ
Richardson, Alan, 41 n. 6, 48 n. 19
Richardson, Cyril, 124 n. 19
Robinson, James M., 62 n. 10, 104, 105 n. 21, 114 n. 36
Romero, Andrés A. Esteban, 36 n. 28

Sacraments, 124–127, 175
Salaverri, Joachim, 102 n. 12

Scheler, Max, 158 n. 20
Schillebeeckx, Edward, 45, 76 n. 42, 98 n. 4, 117 n. 4, 122 n. 15, 124 n. 18, 178 n. 25, 180 n. 1
Schmaus, Michael, 128 n. 26, 144 n. 21, 161 n. 25, 185 n. 10
Schmidt, Wilhelm, 163 n. 3
Schnackenburg, Rudolf, 60 n. 7, 86 n. 17, 136 n. 6
Scholastic theology, 23, 25, 31, 82
Schoonenberg, Peter, 152 n. 9
Self-donation of God, 44, 52, 59f., 97, 120, 132, 143, 149f., 166, 183
Semmelroth, Otto, 136 n. 8
Senses of Scripture, 32, 51, 104; fuller sense of, 51, 104–106
Source of revelation, 17, 59, 95, 110
Stanley, David, 103 n. 14, 114
Stuhlmueller, Carroll, 100 n. 7
Supernatural, 42, 59, 98, 118, 143; natural and, 129, 150; orientation of man, 165–167; world order, 168f.

Tavard, George, 59 n. 4, 110 n. 28
Teilhard de Chardin, Pierre, 148 n. 1
Temple, William, 165 n. 7
Theology, nature of, 20, 24, 37, 139; Scripture and, 138
Thomas Aquinas, St., 82 n. 10, 113 n. 35, 126 n. 22
Thomistic philosophy, 82, 93, 174, 183
Tradition, 109f.; assumption of Mary and, 32; Church and, 109, 128; Old Testament and, 99f.; primitive Church and, 101,